Teach for
Authentic
Engagement

ASCD MEMBER BOOK

Many ASCD members received this book as a
member benefit upon its initial release.

Learn more at: www.ascd.org/memberbooks

Teach for
Authentic
Engagement

LAUREN
POROSOFF

Arlington, Virginia USA

2800 Shirlington Rd., Suite 1001 • Arlington, VA 22206 USA
Phone: 800-933-2723 or 703-578-9600 • Fax: 703-575-5400
Website: www.ascd.org • Email: member@ascd.org
Author guidelines: www.ascd.org/write

Penny Reinart, *Deputy Executive Director;* Genny Ostertag, *Managing Director, Book Acquisitions and Editing;* Susan Hills, *Senior Acquisitions Editor;* Mary Beth Nielsen, *Director, Book Editing;* Jamie Greene, *Senior Editor;* Thomas Lytle, *Creative Director;* Donald Ely, *Art Director;* Masie Chong, *Senior Graphic Designer;* Lisa Hill, *Graphic Designer;* Kelly Marshall, *Production Manager;* Christopher Logan, *Senior Production Specialist;* Circle Graphics, *Typesetter;* Shajuan Martin, *E-Publishing Specialist*

Copyright © 2023 ASCD. All rights reserved. It is illegal to reproduce copies of this work in print or electronic format (including reproductions displayed on a secure intranet or stored in a retrieval system or other electronic storage device from which copies can be made or displayed) without the prior written permission of the publisher. By purchasing only authorized electronic or print editions and not participating in or encouraging piracy of copyrighted materials, you support the rights of authors and publishers. Readers who wish to reproduce or republish excerpts of this work in print or electronic format may do so for a small fee by contacting the Copyright Clearance Center (CCC), 222 Rosewood Dr., Danvers, MA 01923, USA (phone: 978-750-8400; fax: 978-646-8600; web: www.copyright.com). To inquire about site licensing options or any other reuse, contact ASCD Permissions at www.ascd.org/permissions or permissions@ascd.org. For a list of vendors authorized to license ASCD ebooks to institutions, see www.ascd.org/epubs. Send translation inquiries to translations@ascd.org.

ASCD® is a registered trademark of Association for Supervision and Curriculum Development. All other trademarks contained in this book are the property of, and reserved by, their respective owners, and are used for editorial and informational purposes only. No such use should be construed to imply sponsorship or endorsement of the book by the respective owners.

All web links in this book are correct as of the publication date below but may have become inactive or otherwise modified since that time. If you notice a deactivated or changed link, please email books@ascd.org with the words "Link Update" in the subject line. In your message, please specify the web link, the book title, and the page number on which the link appears.

PAPERBACK ISBN: 978-1-4166-3209-2   ASCD product #123045
PDF EBOOK ISBN: 978-1-4166-3210-8; see Books in Print for other formats.
Quantity discounts are available: email programteam@ascd.org or call 800-933-2723, ext. 5773, or 703-575-5773. For desk copies, go to www.ascd.org/deskcopy.

ASCD Member Book No. F23-8 (July PSI+). ASCD Member Books mail to Premium (P), Select (S), and Institutional Plus (I+) members on this schedule: Jan, PSI+; Feb, P; Apr, PSI+; May, P; Jul, PSI+; Aug, P; Sep, PSI+; Nov, PSI+; Dec, P. For current details on membership, see www.ascd.org/membership.

Library of Congress Cataloging-in-Publication Data

Names: Porosoff, Lauren, 1975- author.
Title: Teach for authentic engagement / Lauren Porosoff.
Description: Arlington, VA : ASCD, [2023] | Includes bibliographical references and index.
Identifiers: LCCN 2023005359 (print) | LCCN 2023005360 (ebook) | ISBN 9781416632092 (paperback) | ISBN 9781416632108 (pdf)
Subjects: LCSH: Curriculum planning. | Classroom environment. | Motivation in education.
Classification: LCC LB2806.15 .P667 2023 (print) | LCC LB2806.15 (ebook) | DDC 375.001—dc23/eng/20230306
LC record available at https://lccn.loc.gov/2023005359
LC ebook record available at https://lccn.loc.gov/2023005360

30 29 28 27 26 25 24 23   1 2 3 4 5 6 7 8 9 10 11 12

Teach for Authentic Engagement

Acknowledgments vii

Introduction: Defining Authentic Engagement 1

PART I: ENGAGING WITH THE CONTENT

Chapter 1: Inclusive Materials 9

Chapter 2: Connective Prompts 27

Chapter 3: Orienting Rituals 45

Chapter 4: Values-Based Task Choice 58

PART II: ENGAGING WITH THEIR WORK

Chapter 5: Affirming Assignments 77

Chapter 6: Empowering Work Processes 94

Chapter 7: Co-Constructed Definitions of Success 113

PART III: ENGAGING WITH EACH OTHER

Chapter 8: Respectful Discussions 131

Chapter 9: Collaboration Protocols 148

Chapter 10: Appreciative Reflection 173

Conclusion: Our Jobs and Our Work 189

References 191

Index 195

About the Author 199

Acknowledgments

Many things get easier the more times I do them, but a few things get harder. Writing books is one of those things. I want to thank the people who didn't let me give up on this one, and when I did give up, got me to un-give up.

Susan Hills worked patiently and generously with me to figure out how to shape my raw ideas into a coherent concept. I proposed several ideas that didn't work, and Susan persisted alongside me until we figured out one that did.

Jamie Greene is a brilliant editor. You know how sometimes a little thing makes a big difference? When Jamie makes even the smallest adjustment, it has a huge impact on clarity and readability. He's also a true collaborator. I've been lucky enough to work with Jamie twice, and I'm a better writer for it.

Conversations with so many people have helped me understand how to design instruction so students connect with the content, their work, and each other. I want to thank Taslim Tharani, Laurie Hornik, and Melanie Greenup in particular, along with all my former colleagues at Fieldston, Maret, and JDS.

I want to thank the educators who have participated in my workshops. No matter what the topic of the workshop was, authentic engagement is the driving force behind it, and I appreciate every educator who makes that their work.

I want to thank all the teachers who made me feel like their classrooms were places where I could authentically engage, especially Judy Dorros and Barbara Silber—may their memories be for a blessing—and Janis Birt.

I can never express enough gratitude for my life partner, Jonathan Weinstein; my children, Kalino Porosoff and Jason Weinstein; and my parents, Leslie and Harold Porosoff; but this is my latest attempt. Thank you for supporting, pushing, and inspiring me every day.

And I want to thank my students. All of them. Always.

Introduction: Defining Authentic Engagement

My first year teaching, I didn't know I was supposed to worry about family conferences. I was super excited to meet the people who were raising the wonderful little humans I got to spend my days with. However, my colleagues described "the parents" with such dread that by the time conference day rolled around, I was freaked out, too. I was most anxious about meeting families of students who had track records of academic, behavioral, or emotional struggle because maybe I was failing to support them, but these conferences went smoothly. We were just people talking about what it meant for students to be engaged in their learning and how we could work together to foster their continued engagement.

My last conference of the day was with Lia's parents. Lia was an academically strong, well-behaved, generally happy student with friends. I welcomed her parents into my classroom, thinking this conversation would be a breeze and then I could go home feeling great about myself and my teaching. After we sat down and exchanged pleasantries, I told Lia's parents that she was doing great and asked if they had any concerns we should discuss. They did have a concern. Their child was an academically strong, well-behaved, generally happy student with friends, so how was I going to make sure she didn't fall through the cracks? I don't remember what I said to Lia's parents; I don't even remember the gist of what I said. I must've said *something*, but the truth is, I didn't know the answer to their question.

The deeper truth is, when I was a student, I was a lot like Lia. I was academically strong, at least according to the standards by which we were assessed. I was generally quiet and well behaved, and the times I got in trouble were for skipping class because, guess what? I didn't feel engaged. I had friends, but I didn't feel like I was part of a learning community where I truly belonged. When my parents met with my teachers, they probably heard a similar story to the one I told Lia's parents, even though I often felt bored, lonely, and empty at school.

As a teacher, I wanted to make sure *all* my students—not just the ones like Lia who reminded me of myself—were authentically engaged in my class. That would become a career-long endeavor. This book represents what I've learned (so far) about how to foster authentic engagement in classrooms and what that might mean for you and your students. Before we get to that, though, I need to define what I mean by *authentic engagement*.

Authentic Engagement Is Active

Engage is a verb, so *engaging* is an action—but whose action is it? We might speak of teachers, lessons, activities, or books that *engage* students, which makes students the passive object. We might also speak of students *engaging* in class. As teachers, instead of looking for ways we can engage students, let's think of ourselves as creating the conditions for students to engage.

This book is about how to design instruction such that students with diverse interests, strengths, needs, identities, and values will be able to connect to their learning. Because engagement is their action, not ours, we can't guarantee that all students will engage. However, we can structure our classes so students know *that* they can engage, *how* they can engage, and *why* their engagement is worthwhile.

Authentic Engagement Is Affiliative

Students can't engage in a vacuum; they need to engage in or with something. The three parts of this book are about designing instruction so students engage with the content (Part I), their work (Part II), and each other (Part III).

Authentic engagement means students are not merely going through the motions of school—studying enough to get good grades and advance to the next level, completing assignments to check them off a to-do list, and remaining more or less indifferent to their peers. Authentic engagement is a choice. It means students choose to bring themselves to their learning, work, and relationships.

That choice can lead to tremendous growth and satisfaction, but it also makes students vulnerable. Authenticity means sharing our experiences, identities, histories, and ideas. It means asking questions and asking for help. Authentic engagement means trying new things without knowing how they'll go. It means making messes and mistakes. It means seeing, hearing, and caring for others—and allowing ourselves to be seen, heard, and cared for.

Authentically engaging with the content, their work, and each other opens students up to frustration, disappointment, embarrassment, fear, longing, and loss—and also joy, enthusiasm, amazement, and hope. Authentic engagement means students feel authentic emotions because something authentically important is at stake for them. If we foster authentic engagement in our classes, we need to be willing to feel whatever we feel when our students feel whatever they feel, because that's what it means to fully live.

Authentic Engagement Makes Academic Learning a Source of *Meaning, Vitality, and Community* in Students' Lives

Decades of research tell us that when students are engaged, their academic achievement improves (Cobb, 1972; Lahaderne, 1968; Lei, Cui, & Zhou, 2018; Li & Lerner, 2011; Newmann, 1992; Skinner, Wellborn, & Connell, 1990).

Academic achievement improves (but doesn't guarantee) a student's ability to get into college, find a fulfilling job, support a family, participate in society, make a positive difference in the world, and build close relationships. In short, students achieve academically so they can build lives filled with meaning, vitality, and community. If our goal is for students to build that kind of life, why make them wait until they're adults to start? Why not start right now?

Student engagement might promote academic achievement, but that's not what engagement is *for*. This book proceeds from the assumption that academic content should be a source of meaning, academic work should be a source of vitality, and academic classes should be a source of community. Finding meaning, vitality, and community is the purpose of engagement—and of school itself.

Using This Book

Each chapter of this book includes practical tools and strategies you can use on their own or in combination to design instruction for authentic engagement. You'll also read stories from my experiences as a teacher and a student to give you a sense of what authentic engagement looks like, what hinders it, and where the tools and strategies came from.

The book is divided into three parts. Part I offers instructional design strategies to help students engage with the content so it becomes a source of meaning in their lives.

- Chapter 1 is about making course materials inclusive so students see themselves reflected in their learning and encounter unfamiliar stories, perspectives, and ideas.
- Chapter 2 discusses how to write prompts that help students connect to the content so they can say something meaningful about it and make it relevant in their lives.
- Chapter 3 describes how to orient students within their own learning by creating rituals to mark transitions between topics.
- Chapter 4 shows how to give students a choice of learning tasks and help them make those choices in accordance with their values.

Part II offers strategies for helping students engage with their work so it becomes a source of vitality.

- Chapter 5 is about how to design affirming assignments that ask students to create things that matter—to them personally and in the world.
- Chapter 6 describes work processes that empower students to make projects intrinsically fulfilling.
- Chapter 7 discusses how students and teachers can co-construct definitions of *success* that reflect established learning objectives as well as what matters to the student.

Part III offers strategies for helping students engage with each other so the class becomes a source of community.

- Chapter 8 describes how class discussions can become a site of actively respectful relationship-building within the group.
- Chapter 9 includes various collaboration protocols that foster academic understanding and interpersonal connection.
- Chapter 10 is about using end-of-activity and end-of-unit reflections that help students appreciate their own learning, one another, and the group as a whole.

There's intention behind how this book is sequenced. Students more easily engage with their work when they feel connected to its content, and they're more able to use learning as a context for building community when they feel like that learning matters. Because each chapter provides some foundation for the next, I would recommend reading them in order. That said, if you start with whichever chapters seem most interesting to you (which, to be honest, is how I usually read professional books), you'll be able to use the tools and strategies in those chapters without having read what came before. Either way, I hope you'll engage as authentically in reading this book as I did in writing it.

PART

I

· · ·

Engaging with the Content

1

Inclusive Materials

Reading books and watching movies in the 80s when I was growing up, I always waited for the girl. The protagonist was usually a boy or man—as in *Star Wars*, *The Phantom Tollbooth*, *The Dark Crystal*, *Tales of a Fourth Grade Nothing*, *The Goonies*—but eventually, the girl appeared. Sometimes she was a love interest, sometimes a rival, sometimes a friend. Sometimes she died. Often, she embodied gender stereotypes and taught me harmful lessons about my reason for existing, but I didn't yet know how to read (or watch) critically for that. I just wanted to see the girl.

It was similar in school. We read boys' and men's stories. Sometimes there was no girl to wait for, like in "The Cask of Amontillado." Sometimes the girl was awful, like Sally in *The Catcher in the Rye*, or she was idealized, like Phoebe in *The Catcher in the Rye*. Sometimes the girl had no name, like Curley's wife in *Of Mice and Men*. As a teenager, I learned to hate the girl, so it's not much of a surprise that I was also learning to hate myself.

It wasn't just in English class. The pictures in all our textbooks rarely showed women, and the few women there were mostly white. Our history books were all about white men leading battles and countries, exploring and stealing lands, inventing technologies, and exploiting other humans for profit. Some chapters may have had a paragraph about women such as "women on the home front" during the Revolutionary War, as if there was only one home front and only one set of things women did. In biology, we read about the passive egg and the heroic sperm, and it wouldn't be until a college course on gender psychology that I read a takedown of that narrative (Martin, 1991)—but by then, I'd internalized what role I was supposed to play in the world.

At least in waiting for the girl, I occasionally saw one. I'm Jewish, and even though the stories of science, mathematics, politics, and music are full of Jews, we didn't talk about them in school. If we learned about them, we didn't learn they were Jewish. You can probably guess the single event I read about in history class that mentioned Jews, but I'll tell you anyway: the Holocaust. The message this imparted? We could study our history only when we were murdered by the millions.

It wasn't just myself I longed to see in my learning. I remember repeatedly saying I wanted to study "other cultures." That phrasing makes me cringe now, but given how thoroughly Black and Brown people had been otherized in the lessons I was taught (starting with when my preschool teacher had us make feather headdresses out of construction paper), it's not a surprise. In every subject, I encountered materials that stereotyped, subjugated, and silenced entire groups of people. "I want to study other cultures" was how I expressed a longing to encounter important perspectives my education had missed or misrepresented.

All students need opportunities to see themselves reflected in their learning *and* encounter unfamiliar ideas and perspectives—but so many have to wait for those opportunities, if they come at all. This chapter is about how to create those opportunities right now by making your course materials more inclusive.

Mirrors and Windows

To borrow a well-known metaphor from education professor Rudine Sims Bishop (1990), students need to encounter materials that serve as mirrors reflecting their own experiences and as windows into unfamiliar ideas and perspectives. Mirrors help students build a healthy sense of self, windows help students understand worlds beyond themselves, and both help students engage with the content.

Although students need both windows and mirrors, some course materials overwhelmingly reflect dominant groups—or they reflect stereotypes of marginalized groups. Bishop (1990) explains the danger of providing too few mirrors: "When children cannot find themselves reflected in the books they read, or when the images they see are distorted, negative, or laughable, they learn a powerful lesson about how they are devalued in the society of which they are a part" (p. ix). Mirrors help students situate themselves in a larger story—of science, mathematics, art, and every other subject. If students never see themselves reflected in academic materials, they might think the content has nothing to do with them and feel like outsiders in their own learning.

Conversely, providing too many mirrors and not enough windows can lead students to believe that *their* story is *the* story. By seeing themselves constantly reflected, students in historically dominant groups (such as boys or white students) might see their own experiences as *right* or *normal* and that anyone who doesn't share these identifiers is *lesser* or *other*. Diverse materials send the message that there isn't only one right way to think, act, and be.

There's a third part of Dr. Bishop's metaphor. Window stories can become "sliding glass doors" when students "walk through in imagination to become part of whatever world has been created or recreated by the author" (Bishop, 1990, p. ix); the student not only *sees* unfamiliar experiences but *empathizes* with the people who live them. Empathizing is an active reading process, not a feature of the story itself. Chapter 2 addresses how teachers can invite students to connect with people, places, and events they learn about—what Bishop might call opening the glass door. For now, we'll focus on mirrors and windows: materials that show experiences like and unlike the students' own.

Full-Length Mirrors and Bay Windows

In the stories I read for school, I rarely encountered people who shared the identifiers that felt central to who I was—and that experience is hardly unique. Bestselling author Nic Stone (2020) describes how she met only three Black characters in the books she read from 8th through 12th grade: Tom Robinson in *To Kill a Mockingbird*, Crooks in *Of Mice and Men*, and Jim in *The Adventures of Huckleberry Finn*. These books are all by white authors and about Black suffering: getting falsely accused of a violent crime (Tom); living in physical anguish and social isolation (Crooks); or being enslaved, imprisoned, shot, and repeatedly betrayed (Jim).

Of these reading experiences, Stone (2020) writes,

> I hated all of it. The stuff I could actually get into as a teen: *Harry Potter* and *Gossip Girl*? I wasn't in it. As far as I knew then, Black girls like me didn't exist in books. And as physics would have it, people who don't exist can't go on adventures or solve mysteries or fall in love or save the universe. Which meant that I, as a nonexistent entity, wasn't capable of any of those things. And I wasn't the only person getting this message. Anyone reading books without me in them was getting it too." (paras. 10–12)

Another bestselling author, Nicola Yoon (2021), distinguishes "issue books" about oppression from "non-issue books" that center people in oppressed groups but are not about their oppression. According to Yoon, non-issue books "afford marginalized people the full measure of their humanity. There is more to them (and their lives) than the painful, heavy issues imposed upon them by society. There is also joy" (para. 20).

The materials we offer students cannot be funhouse mirrors that reflect and reinforce stereotypes. The windows cannot be tiny peepholes that show only pain and oppression. Truly inclusive materials offer full-length mirrors and wide bay windows to show a range of experiences—pain and struggle as well as joy and triumph.

Intersectional Inclusivity

As a high school senior, I took a women and literature elective. The reading included one book by an indigenous woman, one by an Asian American woman, one by a Black woman, one by a Latina, and a fifth book we each chose for ourselves. I took that class only three years after Kimberlé Crenshaw (1989) coined the term *intersectionality* to describe how legal discourse excludes Black women's experiences by focusing on either racism or sexism but not on how their combined effect fundamentally differs from each one on its own. People now use the word more broadly, referring to how various aspects of our identities—race, gender, sexuality, socioeconomic class, age, and so on—interact to shape our experiences.

As windows, intersectional materials help students push past biases about particular groups and about the discipline itself. My Women and Literature teacher had selected our course texts to ensure we didn't equate stories with *men's* stories, or women's stories with *white* women's stories. By reading intersectional women's literature, we developed a more expansive understanding of women—and of literature.

As mirrors, intersectional materials help students with diverse backgrounds and identities see different aspects of themselves reflected in the same story. Many years after I'd taken that women and lit course in high school and I was teaching 7th grade, my students read *A Raisin in the Sun*, in which the characters Lena, Beneatha, and Ruth Younger offer three very different portrayals of Black women's strength, vulnerability, and joy. Black girls might see themselves reflected in one or more of the characters, but Black students of other genders and girls of other racial identities might recognize aspects of themselves, too.

Even if a story reflects many aspects of a student's identity, it might not reflect *them*. A story about a white Jewish woman writer in her mid-forties living in the suburbs with her two children isn't necessarily about *me*. (In fact, the show *Girlfriends' Guide to Divorce* was about a white Jewish woman writer in her mid-forties living in the suburbs with her two children, and I can assure you, it was not about me.)

Conversely, almost any story will have *something* that feels familiar. Nic Stone (2020) mentions *Gossip Girl* as a book she, a Black girl in Georgia, "wasn't in." I can't say I see myself in a story about ultra-wealthy teenage Manhattanites, either, but that doesn't mean I have *nothing* in common with those characters. I've had friendship betrayals, unrequited crushes, and selfish tantrums. These parts of *Gossip Girl* are relatable, even if the wealth and access are less so.

To be clear, the fact that almost any student can find something familiar in almost any story does not make it OK that Nic Stone encountered only three Black characters in five years' worth of school books. Teachers have a duty to incorporate culturally sustaining stories into every course *and* to realize our students won't always relate to our course materials in the ways we expect.

Local and Current Inclusivity

Learning materials should reflect not only *who* the students are (identity) but also *where* they are (local environment) and *when* they are (present moment). Before I taught 7th grade English, I taught geography at a different school that had a robust service learning program. Each grade did a project that met a community need and pertained to one of their academic classes. For example, if 8th graders were learning elements of critical literacy in their English class, then their service learning project might be to create critical reading questions they can use to discuss picture books with younger buddies. The 8th graders deepen their critical reading skills as they prepare for and have these conversations, and the younger children get to select books, receive one-on-one attention, and develop their own literacy skills. By working together, the students and their buddies get to know each other, link their communities, and make literacy more accessible.

As a 7th grade teacher, I wanted my students' service learning experience to feel meaningful. My predecessor at the school had been involved with an organization that led landmine removal efforts in Southeast Asia and southern Africa, and she'd created a service project that benefited the organization and aligned with the geography course.

As important as landmine removal is, I was concerned that the service learning project reinforced stereotypes of Southeast Asia and southern Africa as war-torn, poor, and in need of white saviors. I also thought service learning was supposed to be hands-on and involve building relationships. We couldn't travel to Cambodia or Angola and remove mines; we could only raise money for the organization that did. I thought it was important for my students, who were learning about people they didn't meet and places they didn't visit, to apply the knowledge they gained in their geography course to local efforts.

My colleague who taught the other two sections of geography had worked for an organization that protects the Chesapeake Bay watershed. By focusing on something closer to home, we could connect sustainability topics our students learned about during the various regional geography units to similar issues with which they were more familiar. For example, when we learned about deforestation in the Amazon during our Latin America unit, we also learned how forest buffers protect the Chesapeake Bay watershed, visited a forest in Virginia, talked to people working to protect local forests, and wrote to congressional representatives who could help. Our service learning project gave students a different kind of mirror—one that reflected their local environment and present moment.

It's Not Just Books

When Rudine Sims Bishop (1990) introduced the mirrors and windows metaphor, she specifically discussed how children need to see themselves in books, but students encounter stories in all kinds of learning materials, all across the curriculum. In their history classes, they hear stories about various people and events. In science, they hear stories of biological, geological, chemical, and physical phenomena—and about the people who make and interpret observations. A lab procedure is a kind of story. The act of sculpting is a story, the finished sculpture tells a story, and the sculpture and sculptor are part of the ongoing story of art. In language classes, when students learn to describe their clothing or ask for change at a store, they're imagining themselves in a story.

Even in math, we have story problems that make the content relevant in the real world—yet that world might not be the one in which students see themselves. Education professor Anita Bright (2016) studied story problems and discovered that although they "are supposed to be the most humanizing part of math education," they often contain assumptions that "perpetuate consumerism, reinforce racist and sexist stereotypes, and maintain classism and unsustainable approaches to the Earth" (para. 3). Bright's examples include calculating cheap wages to hire migrant workers, the area to recarpet a home, and the calories in a breakfast consisting of foods typically eaten by white Americans.

Math problems, photographs, videos, websites, maps, posters, and games tell stories. The spaces students visit on field trips tell stories. What mirror and window stories did you encounter as a student? How did these stories affect your sense of self and belonging? What did that mean for your engagement in your classes? If you imagine your students at your age now looking back on your class, how would you want them to answer these questions?

The Willingness to Critically Self-Reflect

I've never met a teacher who actively sought out instructional resources *because* they were by and about white cishet men, yet many (if not most) courses overrepresent these voices or treat them as *normal* and everyone else as *other*. Even those of us who believe in equity and inclusion have biases when choosing and using instructional materials, which is why Figure 1.1 offers a set of critical reflection questions you can use to assess them.

You might feel uncomfortable at the thought of questioning your materials. You might worry that you'll find evidence of bias and wonder what that says about you. You might dread the effort it will take to change.

FIGURE 1.1
Critical Reflection Questions About Instructional Materials

Looking at your course materials:

- Whose voices are predominant?
- Whose voices are present but not predominant?
- Whose voices are absent?
- What beliefs about what's "good," "right," or "normal" do these materials reflect?
- Where do those beliefs come from?
- How might these materials inform a student's sense of self and belonging?

Looking at a historically marginalized group:

- What kinds of stories do your course materials tell about this group?
- Do the materials represent this group in rich, affirming, and accurate ways, or do they reinforce subjugation and stereotypes?
- How do your course materials actively challenge stereotypes?

Looking at the students in your class:

- Which aspects of themselves will they see reflected in their learning?
- How will they see their local community represented?
- How will they see current events and issues represented?
- How might their identities inform their learning and work?

Source: Copyright 2023 by Lauren Porosoff.

Maybe you're thinking you'll skip the assessment, telling yourself your materials are already inclusive. Maybe you feel angry because you think I'm implying your class must be racist or sexist or transphobic. Maybe you're rolling your eyes: "Not *this* again."

Maybe you feel fine for now, but as you reflect, you feel uncomfortable emotions such as embarrassment, guilt, or despair. Maybe you find yourself not wanting to write certain things down or pushing those thoughts out of your mind. Maybe you even have uncomfortable physical sensations such as muscle tension or queasiness.

Psychology professor Kelly Wilson eloquently explains that "values and vulnerabilities are poured from the same vessel" (Wilson & DuFrene, 2009, p. 8). The very things that matter most to us are also sources of our deepest pain and our greatest struggles. If, as you assess your instructional materials, you have any uncomfortable thoughts, emotions, or physical sensations, notice them, because they mean you're getting close to something important. What is that something? What will you choose to do? How will your choice affect your students? How satisfying will it ultimately be for you?

Functional Replacement

When I moved to a new school, one of my first acts as an English teacher was a math problem. I looked at the stack of books I'd been charged with teaching and wondered, of all the pages my students would read that year, how many were written by white men? The answer was 74 percent.

The most egregious offender was a book called *21 Great Stories*. All 21 were written by white men. We also read *Of Mice and Men* (white male author, white male protagonist), *The Catcher in the Rye* (white male author, white male protagonist), and *A Midsummer Night's Dream* (which, despite some interesting theories about Shakespeare, was most likely by a white male author, too). The remaining two books were *A Raisin in the Sun* (Black female author, Black family of protagonists) and *I Am the Darker Brother* (an anthology of poems by Black poets).

As I approached my second year in that teaching position, I wanted to make some changes to our course materials, beginning with *21 Great Stories*. Instead of simply ditching it, though, I asked myself what functions the book served—what the book *did*—regardless of whether those functions were intentional or explicit. I came up with six functions:

- Providing access to "classic" literature and famous authors (implicit but probably intentional).
- Teaching students to identify and analyze key themes in stories (explicit and intentional).
- Teaching students to compare and contrast different authors' styles (explicit and intentional).
- Helping students use great texts as models for their own writing (explicit and intentional).
- Appeasing parents who complain that the middle school curriculum is too easy (implicit but probably intentional).
- Sending the message that "great" stories are by and about white men (implicit and probably unintentional).

Of the functions I identified, some were helpful in teaching students important reading and writing skills, some were harmful in perpetuating oppressive systems and ideologies, and some seemed more or less neutral (if anything in education can be). Of the helpful functions, the two that felt most important were teaching students to identify and analyze key themes in stories and helping students use great texts as models for their own writing. I looked for another book that could serve these same two functions but that was by and about people who belonged to a historically underrepresented group. I came up with Sandra Cisneros's *The House on Mango Street*, which is by a Latina author and features a Latina protagonist.

My next step was to list all the functions *The House on Mango Street* could serve, beginning with the two I'd already identified. Here's what I came up with:

- Teaching students to identify and analyze key themes in stories.
- Helping students use great texts as models for their own writing.
- Providing a relatable coming-of-age story for students who are roughly the same age as the main character.
- Guiding students to write about people, events, and things that matter to them.

- Appeasing parents and colleagues who want students to read "classic" literature.
- Sending the message that Latina stories matter.

When I compared my functional analyses of *21 Great Stories* and *The House on Mango Street*, I found that *The House on Mango Street* served more functions my school community and I would deem helpful. I didn't want to make teaching choices for the sake of appeasement but was honest with myself that the book would serve this function. More importantly, it would offer my Latina students a mirror the course had lacked. Providing a mirror for Latina students, and providing a window into Latina experiences for students who didn't so identify, is more than just an added bonus. It is itself an important function of learning materials.

The following protocol is designed to help you do a functional analysis of your course texts or other resources. You'll list all the functions the resource serves, identify the most important functions, and think of another resource that serves those same functions but represents a group that has been stereotyped, subjugated, or silenced in the curriculum.

Functional Replacement Protocol

1. Identify a learning resource you're willing to reconsider and potentially replace—a book or anything else students encounter as they learn the content.
2. Identify all the functions that resource serves. What does it *do*? Some functions will be intentional; that's what you're trying to accomplish. Others will be unintentional; that's not what you were aiming for, but the resource has that impact. Some functions will be explicit; you've stated it out loud or in written communication. Others will be implicit; you never actually state the function, but it exists.
3. Classify the functions as helpful, harmful, or neutral.
4. Of the helpful functions, identify the one or two you consider most important.
5. Find an alternative resource that fulfills those most important helpful functions *and* that is by and about people from a historically underrepresented group. These groups might include Black, Indigenous,

Asian, Pacific Islander, Latine, LGBTQIA+, Jewish, Muslim, Hindu, atheist, disabled, neurodivergent, chronically ill, immigrant, poor, elder individuals or communities, or any other historically under-represented group.

6. Identify more of the new resource's functions—what the new resource *would do.*

7. Identify the functions that serve your values as a teacher and school community member.

What you or anyone else considers most important depends on values. You always bring your personal values to everything you do, including the selection and use of instructional materials. Your values don't exist in a vacuum, though, so you might think about the values of various communities to which you belong: your school, professional organizations, and cultural communities. If you want more perspectives, ask a trusted colleague to do this protocol with you.

Finding Resources

Teachers often have trouble finding resources by members of underrepresented groups because they're just as underrepresented by publishers as they are by schools. Try searching a library catalog or social media site using keywords such as *lesson plan* or *learning resource,* along with your subject and the group you're looking for. Keep in mind, though, that anyone can post anything—including resources that look like meaningful representation but in fact reinforce stereotypes and perpetuate myths. It's a good idea to look for conferences, websites, and online communities where members of historically underrepresented groups discuss instructional resources by and about your subject or grade level.

You might also find inclusive materials in unexpected ways. One of the best books we used in my English class came from a science teacher. She was driving to school one morning and heard an NPR story about the then-new book *Poetry Speaks Who I Am* (Paschen & Raccah, 2010). Its poems by diverse writers were all about identity in one way or another, and the book came with a CD of the poets reading their work.

I taught a unit called Poetry with Purpose that had students explore what poems do and how poetic devices help communicate an idea and establish the poet's voice. After reading and discussing various poems, students tried out the poetic devices they'd explored in their own poems, which they assembled into their own collections.

Poetry Speaks Who I Am provided many excellent, accessible poems we could explore in all these ways. Although the poetry book we had been using, *I Am the Darker Brother*, offered important examples of classic Black poetry, most of the poets were men and no longer alive, and too many of the poems were about Black suffering. I wanted my students to read about diverse experiences—painful *and* joyful—from diverse and mostly living poets. *Poetry Speaks Who I Am* had an introduction students could use as a model when writing introductions to their own collections, and they could record selected poems that I could assemble into a class CD (which later became a class playlist).

A science teacher suggested a great resource for an English unit. Just imagine how many excellent resources your colleagues might know about, even if they teach a different subject or grade level. The following protocol (adapted from Porosoff, 2020) is designed to draw on the collective knowledge of your faculty so you can all discover learning resources that might serve as mirrors and windows for your students. You'll need index cards, lots of sticky notes in four different colors, and pens.

Resource Crowdsource Protocol

1. Each teacher gets an index card and three sticky notes in each of four colors (for a total of 12 sticky notes).
2. Each teacher writes a unit topic on the index card.
3. Each color sticky note is assigned to one of the following four categories of resources.

    People: Whose expertise could help students learn about this topic or pursue this inquiry? Consider experts of all kinds, including those in the students' families and in historically marginalized groups.

    Places: Where could students go to learn about this topic or pursue this inquiry? Consider places on school grounds and in your area.

Think of nearby places your students or their families visit or that have cultural, historical, or ecological significance.

Texts: What could students read or view as part of this unit? Consider all types of verbal, visual, and audiovisual texts, both in print and online, such as fiction and nonfiction books, magazine articles, poems, data sets, works of art, and videos.

Activities: What could students do to discover the content for themselves? How could they deepen their thinking about it? Consider activities of all kinds, such as writing, conducting an experiment, playing a game, dramatizing an event, and making art.

4. Teachers leave their index cards on their desks or tables and walk around the room, looking at the topics and essential questions on each other's cards. They suggest resources for their colleagues' units by writing their own ideas on the appropriate sticky notes and sticking them near each card.

5. The process continues, ideally until each teacher has no sticky notes left and each index card has three sticky notes in each color beside it.

6. Teachers return to their own index cards and read the suggestions.

7. The group debriefs using the following discussion prompts:

— Of all the resources your colleagues suggested, which are you most excited to explore? What can that excitement tell you about your values?

— Of all the resources your colleagues suggested, which is most different from what your students usually encounter in your class? How might they benefit from encountering it?

— Of all the resources you suggested, which do you most hope a colleague will actually use? What can you learn about your values from the fact that you hope your colleague uses that resource?

Any resource that meaningfully advances students' understanding is potentially useful. Look out for cultures and perspectives typically left out of your subject's narrative when you have conversations with students and their families, explore local environments, and follow current events.

When you find instructional resources, notice how you judge them. Which resources do you consider *good*, and which resources do you dismiss as *inappropriate* or *unworkable*? What can those judgments tell you about your own beliefs regarding goodness, appropriateness, and workability? Where do those beliefs come from?

Asking yourself these questions helps you develop what educator Liza Talusan (2022) calls an "identity-conscious practice," which means constantly noticing "that who you are informs and impacts how you act, how you interact with others, and how you see the world around you" (p. 18). Although we might focus on how our course materials reflect our *students'* identities, our own identities shape the ways we select materials in the first place.

Interrogating Materials Selection Systems

By the time I moved from 7th grade English to 6th, the course materials were much more inclusive than they had been. In addition to replacing *21 Great Stories* with *The House on Mango Street* and *I Am the Darker Brother* with *Poetry Speaks Who I Am*, we replaced *The Catcher in the Rye* with Francisco X. Stork's *Marcelo in the Real World*, which features a neurodivergent protagonist, to anchor a unit about personal journeys.

We kept *A Raisin in the Sun* and had students write their own dramatic scenes based on personal experiences with injustice. We also kept *A Midsummer Night's Dream* and *Of Mice and Men* out of fear of what parents would say if we removed them. We added two books by Asian authors: Salman Rushdie's *Haroun and the Sea of Stories*, which anchored a unit that had students write their own fantasy stories based on true learning experiences, and Marjane Satrapi's *Persepolis*, a memoir written in graphic vignettes. Students created a graphic adaptation of one vignette from the collection they'd written after reading *The House on Mango Street*.

Although our booklist wasn't perfect, I'm proud of the changes we made. Seventh graders were encountering mirrors and windows they hadn't encountered before. However, making the changes took eight years—long enough for hundreds of students to pass through 7th grade having never seen themselves in their learning.

As you work to make your own instructional materials more inclusive, it's important to root out why it's exclusive in the first place. What systems are in place that make it less likely for certain students to see themselves reflected?

At my school, one requirement was for students who had different teachers to have "similar experiences." The logic was that it shouldn't matter which teacher a student had for any particular course; the school should be able to guarantee a certain experience. That might sound like an equity-based practice, but "similar experiences" didn't mean all students had to have equivalent opportunities to develop certain understandings and skills; it meant teachers of the same course had to give the same major assignments and use the same materials. For me, it meant I couldn't use a book unless my colleague who also taught 7th grade English used it, too.

That might have been fine if he and I were both open to change and both valued inclusion. However, my colleague had been at the school teaching the same books for many years, and he resisted any book I suggested. That, too, might have been fine if our policy had been for each teacher to choose an equal number of books on each year's list. Instead, the books remained the same from year to year unless everyone teaching the course agreed to a change. If I—an experienced teacher but new to the school—couldn't convince my white male colleague to do otherwise, his white male-authored book choices stayed in place, and I had to use them.

After that colleague left the school, my new grade-level partner and I were able to make changes, but we encountered a new obstacle. We were discouraged from changing more than one or two books from any given year to the next. This unofficial policy existed for two reasons: to save teachers from having too much preparatory work (which I would have gladly taken on so my students could have more mirrors and windows) and to appease powerful parents who expected their children to have certain literary experiences.

In addition, if we wanted to use a different book, we had to submit a written proposal explaining and justifying the change. This policy was an important procedural safeguard against frivolous changes to a booklist that helped our students become more skillful readers, writers, and thinkers, and it prevented us from adding books we liked into the required reading list without considering what students would learn. However, if we wanted to keep a book, we did not have to write anything or justify its continued use. Change required labor that maintenance of the status quo didn't, and if the status quo is overwhelmingly white, male, cisgender, heterosexual, Christian, able-bodied, and neurotypical, then barriers to change are problematic.

Our booklist's evolution demonstrates what educator Paul Gorski (2019) calls "pacing for privilege" (p. 57), or changing slowly enough that those with power remain comfortable, even if it means denying justice to those who have been marginalized. In this case, school policies operated to keep our mostly white population of adults happy—and deny mirrors to the very students who felt most invisible in their own learning.

We can't just ask how to make our resources more inclusive; we also need to ask what systems perpetuate exclusion. Figure 1.2 offers a set of critical reflection questions you can use to assess the process by which your instructional materials are selected.

FIGURE 1.2
Critical Reflection Questions About the Process of Selecting Instructional Materials

In conversations about instructional materials:

- Which voices are heard and taken seriously?
- Which voices are heard but not taken as seriously?
- Which voices are never heard?

In evaluating instructional materials:

- What criteria are used to determine whether to use a particular resource?
- What beliefs about what's "good," "right," or "normal" do these criteria reflect?
- Where do those beliefs come from?

In deciding whether to use instructional materials:

- What is the process for proposing and vetting new resources?
- What is the process for reviewing resources that have been used before?
- What is the process for making decisions? For example, must decision-makers reach consensus? Do they vote? Do they split up the decision-making, each choosing some materials?
- Why are these the processes your school uses?
- What's the impact of these processes? Who benefits from them and who loses out?
- What factors or policies prevent changes in instructional materials?
- Who can help you think of creative workarounds within the existing policy or advocate for changes to the policy itself?

Making our materials more inclusive might cost us time, labor, money, and relationships with those who maintain the status quo. I wish I could take away these costs, but I can't. I can only ask you: What are the costs of *not* making your materials more inclusive—to your students' engagement in your class and to their sense of self and belonging? What are the costs to your colleagues who have less historical and institutional power if you don't take risks to fight for inclusion? What are the costs to you?

Onward

This chapter was about how to engage students by providing instructional materials that both reflect their own experiences and show them unfamiliar ideas and perspectives. As important as inclusive materials are, they don't guarantee our students will connect to the content. The next chapter is about how to help students locate themselves in their learning and make their learning relevant in their lives.

2

Connective Prompts

My family loves to go hiking. (Real hikers would probably call what we do *walking*, but we say we're hiking.) When we first started hiking at the nature preserve near our home, we always took the blue trail. A mile and a half of mostly flat terrain, the blue trail was perfect for my 5-year-old son, Jason, and his out-of-shape mom. The blue trail circled a lake, which was home to all kinds of animals. Walking the same path over and over meant we knew which logs the turtles frequented and how to find a muskrat by watching lily pads for movement.

We loved the blue trail. However, my husband, Jonathan, got bored of it and started making a case for hiking anywhere *but* the blue trail. Over Jason's protests, we tried out the hilly red trail and the too-long orange trail and the too-steep yellow trail. Sometimes we'd even go to other parks, but we always alternated these excursions with hiking the blue trail, to Jason's delight and Jonathan's disappointment.

Until something changed. Maybe it was pandemic-induced desperation, but Jonathan developed a sudden interest in mushrooms. He started learning the names for different mushrooms, how to tell similar-looking ones apart, which were most sought after by chefs, and which were trying to kill you. As it turned out, the trail that had the most mushrooms in the widest variety was the blue trail. While Jason and I searched the lake for animals, Jonathan searched the woods for mushrooms, which he'd identify and tell us about. Suddenly, instead of dreading the blue trail, he couldn't wait to hike it.

The trail itself had not changed. It was the same-old-same-old blue trail, but Jonathan's *experience* of the trail changed when he connected it to a new interest. Psychologists have a fancy name for this process of changing one's experience of a thing without changing the thing itself: transformation of stimulus function (Hayes, Barnes-Holmes, & Roche, 2001). For Jonathan, the blue trail had functioned as a source of boredom, but when he associated it with mushrooms, which functioned as a source of joy, the blue trail took on that function.

By associating something with sources of meaning in our lives, we change our psychological experience of that something so it becomes meaningful, too. This chapter is about how to help your students connect the content of your course to their interests, identities, and values so the course can become a source of meaning in their lives.

Locating a Student's Interests in Our Courses

For Jonathan, connecting the blue trail to a source of meaning was fairly easy. All he had to do was look down, and there were the mushrooms. Connecting course content to student interests is often harder.

Imagine that a younger version of Jonathan is in your class and already has an interest in mushrooms. Would he encounter them in your course content? If you teach life sciences, maybe your students spend a few days on fungi. If you teach literature, maybe mushrooms make a passing appearance in a poem or novel. Now that I think about it, when my students read *The House on Mango Street* and I taught a lesson on similes, one example I used was, "Dead cars appeared overnight like mushrooms" (Cisneros, 1991, p. 17). I doubt one simile would make a student who's interested in mushrooms feel connected to the book, though, and if it did, would that help him engage with the literature or just distract him?

Maybe you teach geometry, and you could write a problem about calculating circumferences of various mushrooms. In order to do that, you'd need to know about Jonathan's interest, but maybe he's never had a chance to talk to you about mushrooms because . . . well . . . it's math class.

This little thought experiment about Jonathan points to several challenges a teacher might face when trying to connect course content to sources of meaning in students' lives:

- Course materials might mention students' area of interest only briefly or superficially, if at all.
- Mentioning students' interests in class might distract them from the content rather than helping them connect to it.
- Even if we were able to meaningfully incorporate students' interests into a lesson or assignment, we don't know about those interests unless a student mentions them.

This last point begs the question: How can we find out what our students are interested in so we can help connect those interests to our course content?

Discovering Our Students' Interests

If we have the sorts of relationships with our students where they feel comfortable talking about their lives beyond school, we might learn about their outside interests—but building relationships like this takes time. It might be April before you've had a conversation during which a student mentions a particular interest, perhaps because it just doesn't come up but especially if mentioning it makes that student vulnerable. I taught a 7th grader who built elaborate sets for imaginative play with action figures, but she didn't talk about them at school because she feared her peers would think it was weird she hadn't outgrown that kind of stuff. Other students might worry that their interests will seem gross, nerdy, or just odd, and even if they feel safe telling *you* all about etymology or medieval diseases or local mushrooms, they might worry that their classmates will overhear and judge them.

Students might feel especially vulnerable disclosing interests that highlight their membership in a historically marginalized group. I had a Mongolian student—I'll call her Urnaa—who one day demonstrated throat singing. No one else in the predominantly white class had heard throat singing before, and although most expressed their curiosity respectfully by asking Urnaa questions and praising her talents, two students started imitating her and snickering. I stopped them as soon as I heard them, and they apologized, but the damage had been done. After that, Urnaa was more cautious about sharing her interests.

To help students share their interests early on—but privately so they feel safer—some teachers give out an interest inventory at the beginning of the year. Many interest inventories ask students about their activities and preferences, some ask about students' homes and families, and some include subject-specific items, such as favorite science topics or authors. Figure 2.1 shows an example of an interest inventory.

Each interest inventory provides a snapshot of one student at one moment in time; we have too many students with too many interests that can evolve and change to be able to keep track of them all. Nevertheless, an interest inventory signals that we care who our students are as whole people who exist outside our classrooms, and it might help us discover ways to connect our content to sources of meaning in their lives.

Overidentifying Students with Their Interests

We've seen how we might struggle to connect students' interests to the curriculum, but we might run into a different kind of trouble when it's easy to make that connection. I had a student—I'll call him Nathan—who liked baseball. His teachers always suggested baseball as a topic for school assignments: "How about Jackie Robinson for your biography?" "You could make your Spanish how-to video about swinging a bat." "For your invention project, what if you imagine a new kind of catcher's mitt?"

I can't claim innocence; when I gave an assignment to write five different poems on a single topic, guess what topic I suggested to Nathan. When he sighed, I asked, "Is that what teachers always tell you to do?" Indeed it was. He ended up writing about his grandparents' farm.

FIGURE 2.1

Student Interest Inventory

Below are questions to help me learn about what's important to you. I want to know you as a person, not just as a student, and I also want to be able to help you make this class meaningful. Please don't feel like you have to answer every question or tell me about parts of your life you'd rather keep to yourself.

Who are some of the PEOPLE who have influenced you or who are a big presence in your life? They might or might not be alive today, and you might or might not have met them in person.	What COMMUNITIES do you belong to? These might be social, cultural, religious, artistic, athletic, activist, or any other group you're a part of.
What PLACES do you feel connected to? These might be ancestral homelands, local hangouts, or places you've visited or hope to visit one day. They might be land or bodies of water.	What TOPICS matter to you? These might be things you like to discuss, read about, watch videos about, or just think about.
What ACTIVITIES do you do? Consider sports, games, visual or performing arts, any other creative endeavor, or any other way you spend your time, whether alone or with others.	What EVENTS are important to you? These might be family events, seasonal events, or milestone events that happened in the past or that will happen in the future.
What ISSUES matter to you? These might be local or global. They might be social, environmental, political, economic, or any other type of issue.	What QUALITIES do you find important in yourself or others? What kind of person do you consider yourself to be or strive to become?

Source: Copyright 2023 by Lauren Porosoff.

Students whose teachers constantly encourage them to incorporate one particular interest into their learning might get bored of that topic after a while. They also might want to keep their out-of-school interests . . . out of school. I've met a lot of students who like baseball, but just because students like to play baseball, or watch baseball, or talk about baseball does not necessarily mean they want to research baseball history or do algebra problems about pitching speed. In some cases, they grow to resent being pigeonholed as "the baseball kid" (or the ballet kid or the mushroom kid). Classrooms are ideal spaces for students to discover and cultivate *new* interests—and to expand who they are beyond any particular interest.

Looking Beyond Student Interests

If we look out for ways to incorporate our students' interests in our courses, we might find opportunities to help students engage more fully. Even if we can't always mushroomify math class or baseballize the biography unit, we should still get to know our students as people, perhaps at first with interest inventories but eventually by building authentic relationships with them. In addition, we can help students build authentic relationships *with the content* by connecting it to themselves. Usually, students won't make those connections automatically. We need to prompt them.

Before we can understand how to prompt students to connect the content to themselves, we need to understand what we mean by *themselves*. Psychologists Dermot Barnes-Holmes, Steven Hayes, and Simon Dymond (2001) describe how people develop a sense of self and the capacity for perspective-taking through *deictic relations*. Here's how that works.

Everything we experience in life, we experience from a unique perspective, which we call *I*. Everything we experience is from a particular location in space, which we call *here*. We experience everything at a particular moment in time, which we call *now*. The words *I*, *here*, and *now* are deictic (a term that comes from the Greek word for *perspective*). Some psychologists refer to *I-here-now* as a single concept because we experience everything as ourselves, in a specific location in space, at a particular moment in time—a perspective.

Understanding *I-here-now* gives us a sense of self and expands our awareness beyond the self. Precisely because we can understand ourselves,

I, we can understand that other people with their own perspectives exist, and we call them *she, he, they*, and so on. (I'll use *they* to represent other people's perspectives because *they* can be singular or plural, and it's gender neutral.) Precisely because we can locate ourselves in space, *here*, we can imagine other locations—near and far, real and fictitious—that we call *there*. And precisely because we can understand ourselves as existing at a moment in time, *now*, we can imagine other moments in the past and future, which we call *then*. Just as *I-here-now* represents the self, the words *they, there*, and *then* represent other perspectives we need to imagine.

Although we experience everything from the perspective of *I-here-now*, we can use our imaginations to change one, two, or all three of those deictic elements, resulting in eight variations:

- *I-here-now:* ourselves in our location at the present moment
- *I-here-then:* ourselves in our location at some other moment in time
- *I-there-now:* ourselves somewhere else at the present moment
- *I-there-then:* ourselves somewhere else at some other moment in time
- *they-here-now:* someone else who is in our location at the present moment
- *they-here-then:* someone else who was or will be in our location at some other moment in time
- *they-there-now:* someone else who is somewhere else at the present moment
- *they there then:* someone else who was or will be somewhere else at some other moment in time

We can use these eight deictic variations to construct questions that help us notice our own experiences (in the case of *I-here-now*) or imagine experiences beyond our own (for all the other deictic variations). Let's try that out. The following questions ask about your experience of reading this book. Answer them, and notice how each one evokes a response from a different perspective:

- As you read this section of the book, what do you notice in your body? (*I-here-now*)

- What were you expecting when you first started reading this chapter? (*I-here-then*)
- If you were doing this exercise in a workshop instead of in a book, how might your experience be different? (*I-there-now*)
- What was your last professional learning experience like? (*I-there-then*)
- Think of one of your colleagues. If that person were reading this book, what would they think so far? (*they-here-now*)
- Who would you most want to discuss this chapter with after you finish reading it? (*they-here-then*)
- What might your students be doing while you are reading this book? (*they-there-now*)
- If you learn how to help your students connect to the content, how will they benefit? (*they-there-then*)

Notice that every question except the very first one includes at least one perspective shift (*they, there, then,* or a combination). The further we get from *I-here-now,* the more we rely on memory and imagination. Notice also that every question except the very last one includes at least one element of our own perspective (*I, here, now,* or a combination). As long as we stay tethered to some element of our own perspective, we can connect ourselves to the world beyond ourselves.

Using Deictic Variations in the Classroom

Just as I can use the deictic variations to construct questions about this book, you can use the deictic variations to construct questions about your course content to help students connect to it. Figure 2.2 has a set of deictic questions about the vignette "My Name" from *The House on Mango Street.* When I first started teaching that book, many students found "My Name" confusing and off-putting; they couldn't understand why the narrator, Esperanza, didn't like her name and wanted a new one.

"Jeez, it's just a name," one student said in exasperation. This was a white boy who'd never heard someone mispronounce his name, and if he was called by the wrong name, it was a mistake, not a microaggression. When I started

FIGURE 2.2
Deictic Questions About "My Name"

I	here	now	How do you feel about your name?
I	here	then	Has someone at school ever called you by the wrong name? How did that feel?
I	there	now	Are you called by other names when you're not at school?
I	there	then	Is there a story about how you were named?
they	here	now	What questions might your classmates have about each other's names?
they	here	then	When is it a microaggression to call a classmate by the wrong name? When is it just a mistake?
they	there	now	Who changes their names? What are some of the reasons people have for changing their names?
they	there	then	Why does Esperanza want to change her name?

Source: Copyright 2023 by Lauren Porosoff.

asking deictic questions, my students were better equipped to understand Esperanza and appreciate the book.

Figure 2.3 presents a set of deictic questions for a unit on lake ecology. Asking questions that move away from *I-here-now* and toward *they, there,* and *then* helps students gradually build a relationship with the topic as they learn about it.

In Figures 2.2 and 2.3, I've included all eight deictic variations for illustrative purposes, but during a unit, we might ask many questions of one type but few (if any) of another. For example, during a unit on the civil rights movement, a history teacher might ask lots of *I-there-then* questions to help students imagine themselves experiencing various events, some *they-there-now* questions to help students connect the civil rights movement to the Black Lives Matter movement, but perhaps only one *I-here-then* question: How did those who fought for civil rights affect your experience at school?

Still, generating questions using all eight deictic variations can help you discover ways for your students to connect the content to their lives. Figure 2.4 offers a planning tool you can use to brainstorm questions for a lesson or unit.

FIGURE 2.3
Deictic Questions About Lake Ecology

I	here	now	What about lake ecology interests you?
I	here	then	What have you learned about photosynthesis in the past?
I	there	now	If you were to visit each lake zone, what would you see, hear, and feel?
I	there	then	Have you been to a lake? Which one? What do you remember about your experiences there?
they	here	now	At home tonight, ask your family members what questions they have about lakes.
they	here	then	How have the lakes in our ecoregion changed over our lifetimes?
they	there	now	If benthic organisms could talk, what questions would we ask them?
they	there	then	If lakes remain healthy over time, who benefits?

Source: Copyright 2023 by Lauren Porosoff.

Meaning-Finding and Meaning-Making

When students encounter an unfamiliar topic in class, they might understandably wonder, "What does this have to do with me?" Deictic questions help students build a relationship with new content by anchoring it to existing sources of meaning in their lives. We might say deictic questions lead to meaning-*finding* since students discover some connection between the topic and their lives.

Another way to help students connect to unfamiliar topics is through meaning-*making*. Students can build a relationship with the content by saying something important about it. Beyond figuring out "What does this have to do with me?" they can also figure out "What do I have to do with this?"

The idea that they could say something important about, say, the Great Depression or the circulatory system might baffle a student who knows very little about these topics and isn't already interested in them. To help students say important things about unfamiliar topics, we can give them evocative texts and exploratory questions.

FIGURE 2.4

Deictic Question Planning Tool

Lesson or Unit Topic:	
Student Response Perspective	**Possible Questions**

I | here | now	
I | here | then	
I | there | now	
I | there | then	
they | here | now	
they | here | then	
they | there | now	
they | there | then	

Evocative Texts

In order to help students find something meaningful to say about the content, first give them a specific text that will help them understand a key topic while also getting them to think, feel, wonder, and imagine. I'm using the word *text* loosely to mean visual or verbal information presented in any format, such as a story, a poem, an essay, a data table, a problem set, a mathematical proof, a comic, a puzzle, a painting, a photograph, a map, a diagram, a speech, a song, or an animation. If the text is a recording, such as a song or speech, students might need a transcript so they can follow along as they listen or go back later to find important parts.

Whatever genre and format you use, a text brings students closer to the topic they're studying. For example, imagine that a history class is studying the Dust Bowl. The Dust Bowl happened *there-then*—at another time and in another place—but students can read a John Steinbeck story *here-now*, in class. Now imagine science students learning about different types of white blood cells. Their own white blood cells are physically present *here-now*, but because the students can't see them, they're not psychologically present. However, a video, a cartoon, or an infographic about white blood cells is both physically and psychologically present. Students can perceive it *here-now* and therefore respond to it.

Diversifying the formats and genres of text through which your students encounter a topic gives them more opportunities to say something meaningful about it. A student learning about the Dust Bowl might respond differently to a John Steinbeck story, a Dorothea Lange photo, and a Woody Guthrie song. The student might have important things to say about all three texts but *different* important things, which ultimately means they've connected to the overall topic, the Dust Bowl, in multiple ways.

Exploratory Prompts

An evocative text might be enough to elicit a meaningful response from some students. However, if our goal is for *all* students to feel connected to the content, then we need to give them prompts that help them say something meaningful. A purely exploratory prompt asks students to notice what the text is (and isn't) saying to them and then say something back.

Consider the following questions about the Remedios Varo (1961) painting *La llamada*:

- What do you see? What *else* do you see?
- The central figure is bright orange, contrasting with the gray and beige colors of everything around her. Imagine one of the paintings we've studied but with this color scheme. How would that painting feel different?
- After the woman finishes walking through the hallway, the people in the walls have a conversation. Write it.

These questions don't ask what the painting means, how to interpret its symbolism, or what the artist might have intended. The last question isn't actually a question; it's a prompt. It's important to note that exploratory prompts don't have right or best answers, which means they don't have wrong or inadequate answers. Exploring isn't something you can do rightly or wrongly; it's something you simply *do*. When I give exploratory prompts, I often say that the only way to do it wrong is to not do it at all.

Good exploratory prompts invite students into the text so they notice their own experience of it and say something back to it. The prompts should be specific enough that students understand exactly what they're being asked to think about and do. Let's look at six types of exploratory prompts. These first three types ask students to look through the text and see what they notice:

- **Collecting Details:** A good way to get students to start exploring is to say, "Make a list of details you notice." Give them time to make their lists, and then ask, "What *else* do you notice? Keep adding to your list." Giving this simple two-part prompt helps students look and then look again. You might follow up by asking them to notice what they noticed the first time and what they noticed when they went back and looked again. If your students are reading a verbal text, consider having them draw the details they notice. Try handing out a grid and having them draw one detail in each square. Drawing means they need to notice concrete things, as opposed to abstract ideas, which can help them connect to challenging material.

- **Acknowledging Absences:** If collecting details helps students notice what's in the text, then acknowledging absences helps them notice what's *not* there. Ask a question such as "What would you expect to see on a map that you don't see on this one?" or "What data *didn't* the author collect?" or "What *isn't* this article about?"

- **Asking Their Own Questions:** Students might assume they can say something meaningful about a topic only if they already understand it, but in every discipline, practitioners make meaning by asking questions. A good way to elicit student questions is to first have them list details and absences, then ask them to notice which ones make them curious or confused. If they're curious or confused, then they have a question—anything from "What's that little squiggly thing?" or "What does *unalienable* mean?" to "Do white blood cells ever attack other white blood cells?" or "If just powers are derived from the consent of the governed, what happens when the governed don't consent?" Often, students will ask questions that could lead to rich discussion—or at least illuminate areas you need to explain. Even if your students don't get their questions answered, just asking is an important way for them to make meaning.

Whereas the first three types of prompts have students look throughout the text, the next three draw students' attention to a particular textual detail or feature so they can say something meaningful about it:

- **Imagining Possibilities:** Most texts include at least one unusual detail: an interesting phrase, a surprising image, a creative metaphor, or something else that stands out. Unusual details are great opportunities to ask unusual questions that free students from their usual ways of responding. They can imagine *possible* meanings rather than trying to guess *the* meaning. For example, when my students were reading *The Catcher in the Rye*, I could have asked them to defend or refute the claim that Holden is just as phony as Sally. That's not a bad prompt, but students aren't creating meaning; they're finding evidence to determine whether my suggested meaning is correct. Instead, I asked, "If Sally is 'Queen of the Phonies,' what is Holden's position in Phonyland?" This question invited students to imagine Holden as King of the Phonies because he's just as phony as Sally, a jester because he's kind of a joke to her, a servant who wants to be free of phoniness but can't help but be phony when he's surrounded by phonies, or in any other role they can dream up. A playful question invites students to come and play, too.

- **Describing Their Psychological Experience:** Our psychological experiences include our thoughts, memories, emotions, and physical sensations. I usually ask students to notice how they experienced a pattern or progression in the text because changes in their thoughts or emotions reveal that something important was happening in the text at that point. For example, my psychological experience prompt about *The Catcher in the Rye* was "This book begins and ends with visits to teachers. Make a timeline of your own emotions as you read about each of these visits." Students have psychological experiences all the time, including when they encounter texts in our classes. The stronger their feelings, the more important that aspect of their encounter is to them. Sometimes students say things like "I have no clue what this is about" or "No offense, but this is just boring." Even confusion and boredom are psychological experiences that students can explore, and through that exploration, they can create meaning.

- **Situating the Text in a Larger Conversation of Ideas:** Any text you give your students is part of a conversation of ideas that goes back generations. When students read the text, they're listening in on the conversation. When they respond, they're joining the conversation. Idea prompts don't necessarily point toward the most obvious themes in the text itself; rather, they provide opportunities for students to connect themes that might be less apparent in the text to themes that matter in their lives, communities, and world. My idea prompt for *The Catcher in the Rye* was "How do race, class, and gender affect Holden's experiences?" Holden doesn't mention these terms, but the ideas are very present in the text—and in students' lives. Larger idea prompts help students relate the unit content to topics they've discussed during previous units, in other classes, and among themselves.

Prompts that ask students to imagine possibilities, describe their psychological experience of the text, and situate the text in a larger conversation of ideas will depend on the text itself. Figure 2.5 offers examples to guide you in developing your own prompts about texts you use (or could use) in your course. I've included texts about topics drawn from various content areas and in various formats and genres. All these texts can be accessed online for free.

Again, the only way to respond wrong to an exploratory prompt is to not respond at all. Sometimes, students *don't* respond at all. When I approach those students, they usually start explaining why they're not writing, and that explanation is a response to the prompt! Let's go back to that question about Holden's position in the land of phonies. Imagine a student sitting at his desk, not writing anything. When I approach him, he whispers, "I don't know what to write. Like, Holden's not a king because a king has self-respect, but he's not, like, a commoner either because not one thing he does is common." There it is. That's what the student should write.

Many questions students hear in school demand a particular kind of engagement: seeking the right or best answer. Exploratory prompts are designed to stimulate *any* kind of meaningful engagement. A perfectly acceptable way to begin responding to an exploratory prompt would be "That's a stupid question." From this, the student could proceed to explain why it's a stupid question to ask about the content, and that counts as saying something meaningful about the content!

Multimodal Responding

Some prompts build in how to respond. When we ask students to make a timeline of their own emotions or draw something in the room as if it had a fractal pattern, they know to respond by making a timeline or drawing. Often, though, the form of their response is independent of the prompt. For example, if I ask how race, class, and gender affect Holden's experiences, a student could write a paragraph, make a list, or draw pictures. Students could respond in conversations with a partner or small group, or they could write a response that they then share—or that they don't share, in which case the purpose of writing was to connect to the content for themselves.

FIGURE 2.5
Example Exploratory Prompts

Text	Prompts		
	Imagine Possibilities	*Describe Psychological Experience*	*Situate in a Larger Conversation of Ideas*
"Theme for English B" by Langston Hughes (2002/1949) (tinyurl.com/yz3t9dfs)	What if it were English A?	Early in the poem, Hughes mentions several locations: cities, neighborhoods, streets, and a building. Pick out a few of these and describe how you felt when you encountered each one in the text.	Who is "somewhat more free" than you? Who are you "somewhat more free" than?
"Latin American Diet Pyramid," "African Heritage Diet Pyramid," "Asian Diet Pyramid" from Oldways Preservation and Exchange Trust (2009, 2011, 2018) (tinyurl.com/47yet3ht; tinyurl.com /mau2mwxn; tinyurl .com/2p8u8dxc)	All three diet pyramids say to base every meal on foods at the bottom. For each pyramid, create a one-day breakfast, lunch, and dinner plan based on the foods at the bottom.	Choose the pyramid you're most drawn to. Annotate it with the images or memories you associate with the foods you see.	According to these images, what makes a diet healthy?
"I Sell the Shadow to Support the Substance" by Sojourner Truth (1864) (tinyurl.com /55s9cxm5)	What's with the period after Sojourner Truth's name beneath the photograph?	How do the thoughts and feelings you have when looking at this photo of Sojourner Truth compare to thoughts and feelings you have when scrolling through photos of people you know?	As a child and young adult, Sojourner Truth was enslaved. After gaining legal ownership of herself, she sold self-portraits to support herself and the abolitionist and suffragist causes she fought for. How can we support her legacy?
How Math Is Our Real Sixth Sense by Eddie Woo (2018) (tinyurl.com /s28sxd56)	Woo shows us how rivers, trees, lightning, and blood vessels share similar geometry. Find something in this room that *doesn't* have that geometry and draw what it would look like if it did.	Woo claims that math "is a sense just like sight and touch" and that it's "our sense for patterns, relationships, and logical connections." Do you believe that?	Woo begins and ends his talk by declaring his love for mathematics. The talk seems like it's about mathematics. How is it also about love?
Landfill Harmonic Movie Teaser by Landfill Harmonic (2013) (tinyurl.com /7pvknud5)	Early in the video (00:34–00:47s), one of the musicians lists the discarded items from which his cello was made. Choose one of these items and tell its story from its perspective.	After watching the video, listen to the audio without watching. What do you notice or think about when you only pay attention to the sounds?	What messages about success can we get from watching this video?

I almost always had my students write or draw responses to exploratory prompts, not only so they had a record of their thinking but also so they could physically see their own thoughts manifesting as words and pictures. They might not realize what they think until they see their own words and pictures on the page, and they can then explore those words and pictures further—thus deepening their thinking. Writing also means every student can respond to the prompt at the same time, as opposed to a discussion in which they take turns.

Occasionally, a student will ask to use a different modality. They say something like "Can I make a mind map instead of a timeline?" or "I *literally* can't draw. Can I just make a list?" Usually when students ask to use a different modality, I explain the prompt's purpose and leave them to decide what to do: "I asked for a timeline so you could notice when and how your emotions changed, but if you feel like a mind map would be a better tool to help notice your emotional response, go for it. Remember . . ." and then they usually join in with me, "the only way to do this wrong is to not do it at all."

Different modalities give students opportunities to create meaning in different ways. Listing emotions I felt while reading about Holden's encounters with his teachers, making a timeline of those emotions, drawing a mind map, writing a paragraph, and choosing emoji to represent my emotional journey will not only elicit different products, they'll elicit different ways of thinking about the content—and offer different ways of connecting to it.

Onward

This chapter was about using connective prompts, which enable students to relate the content to their lives, bring themselves to the content, and express their own ideas through various modalities. In the next chapter, we'll see how to use learning rituals to help students orient themselves within a unit so they can better connect to its content.

3

Orienting Rituals

My older child went to a baby gym where every class started with "Welcome, welcome everyone, we are here to have some fun" to the tune of *Twinkle Twinkle Little Star*. My younger child took a baby music class where the group leader sang each child's name—"Hello Jason, it's good to see you"—and so on through the whole group, no matter how long it took. I wasn't the only caregiver who found these welcoming songs annoyingly catchy, but they orient small children: An important event is beginning *now*, the group is assembling *here*, and *you* are an integral part of our learning community.

Welcoming songs mostly disappear from classrooms by the time children are old enough to read and write. (Maybe we can imagine a Netflix comedy where an algebra teacher starts class by singing to each of her 10th graders. I'd watch that show.) However, just because welcoming songs aren't appropriate for older students doesn't mean they no longer need rituals.

Researcher Caitlin O'Connell (2021) explains that rituals enable people "to survive in a very complex world, to predict what will happen next, and to connect deeply with their families and communities" (p. 5). As students get older, the ritual's form needs to change, but its functions still matter. Classroom rituals communicate three messages to students:

1. **Learning this is important.** A ritual helps us bring greater awareness to the action we're about to perform—in this case, learning—and inspires respect for that action. So much can capture students' attention, and a classroom ritual tells them to focus on learning, not necessarily because that day's lesson is flashy or fun but because the content matters.

2. **Today's learning is part of a larger pattern.** Philosopher Byung-Chul Han (2020) explains that rituals "are to time what a home is to space" (p. 2). What Han calls the "self-sameness" of rituals makes them familiar (p. 3). Even as students learn new content, the ways they encounter that content should be predictable enough that students feel safe exploring, experimenting, asking questions, and making mistakes.

3. **We're in this together.** Performing a ritual together helps build a sense of community. Engaging in a classroom ritual together not only orients students toward their learning, it helps them see themselves as part of a learning community.

When to Use Classroom Rituals

Many rituals mark some kind of transition—from being apart to being together, from being away to being home, from the everyday to a holiday, or from one life stage to the next. In classrooms, students often transition from one topic to another within a unit, such as going from organelles to mitosis in a unit about cell biology, or they transition from one unit to another, such as going from a cell biology unit to a genetics unit.

Some classes transition without any sort of ritual; students simply turn the page to a new chapter in their textbooks with no action to signal something new and important is about to happen. Even if most students move on to a new topic easily, some might get a little lost. "Wait . . . is this about cells?" Others might simply follow instructions and never wonder how one day's topic connects to the previous day's—or why any of the topics matter.

They might understand a learning task as a discrete event ("We're watching a video on mitosis") but not as building toward a larger understanding. Rituals can orient students to new topics and connect them to old ones so they can more fully engage in learning.

The rest of this chapter describes various rituals to mark transitions between topics so students feel more connected to their learning. If these rituals don't seem like they'd work for your students, modify the language and pacing, omit or rearrange certain steps, add your own components, or combine them with other rituals you already use. You can even ask your students for feedback and design rituals together. Do whatever works to help your students understand, "Here we are together. This is what we're learning. Learning it matters."

Transitioning to a New Unit

A *unit* is a timebound study of a particular topic, such as a week about haiku, a month about polynomial functions, or a trimester about media literacy. Units consist of *tasks* that are carefully sequenced to build on one another and progress toward a learning *outcome*—what students will ultimately understand and be able to do regarding the topic. During a unit, students usually engage with a distinct set of resources, such as a particular novel, series of videos, or textbook chapter. Many units involve creating some sort of *product* or *performance*, such as an essay, a podcast, a board game, an art exhibition, or an infographic.

Some teachers begin units by simply stating its topic ("Today we're starting *Hamlet*") and plunging into the first learning task ("Open your book to Act One, Scene One. We need a Francisco and a Bernardo.") Others introduce the unit topic and ask students what's familiar and unfamiliar about it. ("Today we're starting a new unit on genetics. What have you heard or read about genes? What questions do you have about genetics?") From there, students move without much ceremony from topic to topic and task to task until they reach the last one, review what they learned, and are assessed. Rituals can help students better understand what they're learning—and why they're learning it—so they feel more connected to it.

Unit Summaries

One way to signal unit beginnings while also preparing students to learn about the topic is to provide a unit summary. Unit summaries do for students what book jackets do for readers and what vacation brochures do for travelers: they help the person imagine their upcoming experience and understand that they'll gain something meaningful from it. Figure 3.1 has a unit summary for a unit on *A Midsummer Night's Dream* from my 7th grade English course.

A unit summary should include

- **Outcomes:** what students will learn during the unit
- **Tasks:** what students will do in order to learn
- **Resources:** what students will use to help them learn
- **A major product or performance:** what students will create in order to reinforce and demonstrate their learning

These pieces of information help students understand what they're about to experience. I also gave each of my units a *number* to indicate where we were in our learning journey and a *title* that indicated the unit's purpose and not just its content. When reading *A Midsummer Night's Dream*, we weren't just a bunch of people who happened to be in the same room at the same time reading the same play; we were engaging in our third academic undertaking together, and this one involved reinventing Shakespeare's text. Giving

FIGURE 3.1
Example Unit Summary

Unit 3: Reinventing Shakespeare

A Midsummer Night's Dream is one of 38 plays written by William Shakespeare. Although Shakespeare lived 400 years ago, his work is still widely read, performed, and reinterpreted. During this unit, we'll first examine and respond to Shakespeare's text. Then we'll watch three different film adaptations, each of which sets the play in a different place, to see how the settings affect choices of costumes, music, lighting, and other aspects of production. After seeing different ways this play has been reinvented in different settings, you'll work in a group to imagine a new setting for the play and build a model of your set. Then, in a group essay, you'll explain how your setting choice would affect the ways the play would be adapted.

Source: Copyright 2023 by Lauren Porosoff.

out a unit summary is a very simple ritual that orients students within their learning and community.

Values Activation

In an anticipatory set, an element of the classic lesson plan template that educator Madeline Hunter (1982) developed, the teacher does something to capture students' attention. Education blogger Jennifer Gonzalez (2014) gives a great example of an anticipatory set for a lesson about hygiene: "You could come into the room, your hair a mess, with dirt under your fingernails, stained clothing, your teeth covered in yellow goo, with little signs taped all over you that say *scabies, diarrhea, hepatitis A, hookworm,* and *lice*" (para. 2). Lest my fellow introverts think teachers must dress up and perform for an anticipatory set, we can also use videos, games, art, and other exciting activities to get our students curious about the topic they're about to study.

That said, we now live in a different world from the one in which Madeline Hunter designed her template. These days, every corporation, influencer, and rando on the street is trying to get our attention. Teachers who use anticipatory sets don't have a profit motive, and awakening students' curiosity ultimately helps them learn. Still, capturing our students' attention before they know why a topic is worth their attention feels a little manipulative—and runs counter to the critical thinking and deliberate action many of us try to foster.

Values activation is different. Here, we're asking questions to help students articulate how their upcoming learning connects to sources of meaning in their lives—and is therefore itself meaningful and worthy of their time and effort. Figure 3.2 includes a list of questions you can ask to activate students' values. Choose two or three to ask at the beginning of every unit so that answering those particular questions becomes its own ritual. To be able to answer questions such as these, students need to know what the upcoming unit entails, which is why values activation works well after students have read a unit summary.

Each time a new unit begins, you can send families the unit summary and the same values-activating questions to discuss at home. A father might start a conversation with his daughter about not only what makes *her* curious

FIGURE 3.2

Example Questions to Activate Student Values

- What about this unit makes you curious?
- What are you learning about in other places—at home, in your other classes, or in your out-of-school life—that this unit relates to?
- What do you hope to have accomplished by the end of the unit?
- How is this unit an opportunity for you to be creative? (You can substitute any quality for *creative*—perhaps *compassionate, responsible, appreciative, trustworthy,* or *playful.* If your school has certain core values, consider using them in this question.)
- Who might experience this unit differently from how you will?
- Why will your future self be glad you learned about this unit's topic or did this unit's work?
- How will your community benefit from you learning about this topic or doing this work?
- Whose legacy does this work help you carry forward?

but also what makes *him* curious about the unit topic. For those who are interested, these questions can serve as a family ritual that extends students' learning and builds a sense that their learning matters—not just for the sake of academic achievement, but in and of itself.

Resource Look

During many units of study, students encounter new resources such as books, laboratory equipment, art materials, or digital tools that help them learn. Even if you use the same textbook all year, each unit will draw from a different chapter.

My students were sometimes excited to start reading a particular book but occasionally found it a little daunting. The first year I taught *The House on Mango Street,* I explained in my unit summary that the book was written in vignettes, yet students struggled with the format when they started reading.

The following year, I started the unit with a "book look." First, students flipped through the pages and wrote down things they noticed. Then I asked how their experience of reading this book might be different from their experiences of books they'd read in the past. We then discussed what might be interesting and challenging about this new experience. The book look replaced students' skepticism with curiosity, helped them face challenges more willingly and sometimes enthusiastically, and created the sense that they were engaging in this interesting, difficult work together. Eventually, I started doing book looks at the beginning of every unit, and they became yet another ritual to foster engagement.

Your unit's major resources might not be books, in which case you can't call this ritual a "book look" (which is too bad if you like things that rhyme), but you can still do a resource look with any new texts, tools, materials, or equipment students will use:

- Give students time to explore or play with a new resource and have them write down things they notice.
- Ask students how they think their experience of using or interacting with this resource might be different from their experiences of other, similar resources they've encountered in the past.
- Discuss what will be interesting—and challenging—about using or interacting with this resource.

A resource look does more than familiarize students with resources they might find inaccessible or strange; it honors the fact that they're newly encountering *this, here, now, together*. The resource look can become a ritual that helps students discover their individual and common interests, frame challenges as positive, and support one another through those challenges.

Transitioning Between Topics Within a Unit

Just as students don't always notice transitions from one unit to another, they don't always notice transitions from one topic to another within a unit. For example, although my students received a summary of our Reinventing Shakespeare unit on the first day (see Figure 3.1), they walked into the classroom on subsequent days not necessarily remembering where we were in our learning. But then, on the board, they'd see a lesson number and title, such as "3.5: How does a director's choice of setting affect the play's meaning?" They'd copy the lesson number and title into their notebooks, now knowing we were up to the unit's fifth lesson, which would be an inquiry into a director's setting choices. In short, setting up each day's notes with a lesson number and title helps orient students to each new topic within a unit.

Writing Lesson Titles

A lesson title's format depends on what kind of lesson it is. Because I taught English, my units had a reading stage, when we read a particular text or set of texts, and a writing stage, when we either wrote about the text, used it as a model for writing the same genre, or wrote about a similar theme. During the reading stage, lessons were inquiry-based; we had discussions and did activities to explore a particular technique, motif, or theme. During the writing stage, lessons were project-based; I taught strategies to help students successfully complete the project, and then they had time to use the strategies, offer feedback on one another's work in progress, and meet with me.

When a lesson is inquiry-based, its title is a question. Students won't necessarily have an answer by the lesson's end; rather, the question serves to provoke observation, interpretation, storytelling, speculation, and more questions. During my Reinventing Shakespeare unit, the inquiry-based lessons included the following:

- 3.8: How do different settings highlight different themes?
- 3.9: Where else could this play be set? What themes might those settings highlight?
- 3.10: How will the setting we chose affect the meaning of this play?

When a lesson is project-based, its title expresses a strategic action that helps students complete the project. The title usually begins with an *–ing* verb that states the action students will perform at that stage of the project, such as *collecting* water samples for a chemistry experiment or *making* an armature for a sculpture. For my Reinventing Shakespeare unit, groups of students reimagined the play in a new setting, built a model of that setting, and collaboratively wrote an essay explaining how and why they'd produce *A Midsummer Night's Dream* in a particular setting. My project-based lessons included the following:

- 3.11: Creating Scenery for the Stage Model
- 3.12: Writing the Essay's Body Paragraphs
- 3.13: Writing Introductions and Conclusions
- 3.14: Assembling the Group Essay

Some lessons are rehearsal-based; that is, students practice a skill to maintain or expand their repertoire. Titles of rehearsal-based lessons usually begin with the words *how to* and then identify skill goals, such as *how to* use the quadratic formula or *how to* cite online sources. These titles inform students of what they can expect to be able to do by the lesson's end.

Figure 3.3 shows examples of inquiry-, project-, and rehearsal-based lesson titles for units in various subjects.

FIGURE 3.3

Example Inquiry-, Project-, and Rehearsal-Based Lesson Titles

Subject	Unit Topic	Inquiry-Based Lesson Title	Project-Based Lesson Title	Rehearsal-Based Lesson Title
Art	Slab Construction	How is slab construction different from coil construction?	Making a template for a slab box	How to use different tools to create slabs
English	*The House on Mango Street*	What does power look like on Mango Street?	Choosing vignettes to include in your collection	How to use fragments intentionally and avoid using them unintentionally
Health	Nutrition	What factors influence our food decisions?	Setting values-based nourishment goals	How to determine nutritional needs
History	The Cold War	What are the features of a totalitarian state?	Coming up with a thesis about a historical event	How to ask open-ended and follow-up questions in an interview
Mathematics	Graphing Functions	Why describe functions verbally, visually, and algebraically?	Presenting functional relationship mini-posters for peer review	How to graph data sets in the coordinate plane
Physical Education	Baseball	What does it mean to "see the ball"?	Filming your how to/how not to video	How to catch a pop fly
Science	Watersheds	Is polluted water the same as dirty water?	Collecting water samples	How to measure water quality using various indicators
Spanish	Finding Our Way Around	What information do people need to navigate an unfamiliar place?	Making direction cards for locations in the school building	How to use prepositions of place

Transitioning Out of a Unit

If most units of study don't begin with much ceremony, then they end with even less. Students take a test, turn in a product, or give a performance, and that's it. Some teachers display student work on classroom walls or in hallways, where it hangs until the students produce more work to take its place.

When important events or time periods end, we need some sort of closure. We might celebrate (birthdays, book launches) or mourn (divorces, deaths) or do both at once (graduations, retirements). Often, during these rituals, we express an intentional choice about what to carry forward from our experience. A unit-closing ritual helps students collectively acknowledge that their learning was worthwhile.

Sensory Experiences

During my second year teaching 2nd grade, while browsing an activity guide to teaching about the rainforest, I came across an idea to have a "taste of the rainforest" event. I loved the idea of introducing new foods, or introducing familiar foods in new ways, by connecting them to the places we'd learned about.

If I remember correctly, the activity guide suggested having students taste three or four foods, but I was in the "go big or go home" phase of my career. I went to the grocery store and loaded up my cart with canned lychees, fresh coconut, tangerine, dark chocolate, coffee (because one sip couldn't hurt), pineapple, guava juice, Brazil nuts, avocado, banana, papaya, and probably more.

I spent a whole evening looking online for pictures of what these different foods look like when they're growing: a pineapple at the center of a spiky bromeliad, cacao pods hanging from a tree, coffee cherries, and so on. I printed out the pictures on cards and added information about the food. My plan was to give each student a card so they could read the information aloud and show the picture to the class, and then everyone would try the associated food.

Looking back, I realize I should've had the students make the information cards themselves. I also should've predicted some of their reactions: "My mom lets me have Starbucks," a girl scoffed when I served her a teaspoon of coffee, to which a boy countered, "I hope this is decaf." They didn't like everything they tasted—most spit out the excellent dark chocolate—and those who had allergies couldn't try all the foods. Still, the experience created a sensory memory that students could carry forward.

A few years later at a different school, I was teaching a 7th grade geography course in which each unit covered a different global region. By that point, I'd read *Beyond Heroes and Holidays* (Lee, Menkart, & Okazawa-Rey, 1998) and was wary of how multicultural food events can reinforce stereotypes, but when used to conclude a meaningful inquiry-based unit, a "taste of" event seemed respectful and fun. We had "Taste of Latin America," "Taste of Africa," "Taste of Europe," and "Taste of East and South Asia." This time, instead of supplying the food, I had students choose simple recipes and make the food themselves. Most students made food for every unit, but there was no requirement or extra incentive to do so.

During our celebrations, we sat in a circle. Each student who'd cooked described the recipe, its geographic origin and cultural significance, and any ingredient or technique substitutions they had to make. They also gave a complete list of ingredients so students could avoid allergens. Once we'd heard about all the dishes, we ate together and shared what we'd found most interesting, challenging, and meaningful from throughout the unit.

Because we repeated this multimodal, multisensory event for each unit, students understood that they were transitioning away from learning about a particular place, yet that learning mattered and could continue to matter in their lives. They also used that moment to reconnect with one another, which would be important as they moved into the next unit.

Units about the rainforest and geographic regions lend themselves easily to food-oriented celebrations, and you might imagine ways to use the "taste of" format in other subjects. However, food might not quite work with your content. (When I taught English at yet another school and lamented to a colleague that I couldn't do "taste of" celebrations with my curriculum, she joked that we could eat oatmeal raisin cookies after *A Raisin in the Sun* and rye bread after *The Catcher in the Rye*.) More importantly, some students don't have access to enough food for themselves and their families, let alone tasting portions for their class, and some don't have family members who can take them shopping for ingredients and supervise them while they cook.

Fortunately, there are other senses besides taste. Music, movement, gallery walks, art making, recitations, and field trips can all make for multisensory rituals to signal unit endings, highlight important learning, and build community.

Unit Clear-Out

Sometimes, several weeks or even months after a unit ends, a student will show the teacher a crumpled handout and ask, "Do we still need this?" To us, it might seem obvious what students should do with old materials, but they often don't know.

Back when my students had binders, I used white paper for handouts they only needed during the unit and green paper for handouts they needed to keep all year, such as writing guides or checklists that transcended any one project. When the unit ended, I'd say, "Keep all green!" By the third or fourth unit, students would say it before I did.

"Keep all green" signaled the beginning of a ritual: the unit clear-out. Students removed white handouts from their binders and recycled them, occasionally deciding to take home a poem they loved or a graphic organizer they'd found especially helpful. I won't pretend that I never saw them gleefully tossing stuff they never wanted to see again, but I also witnessed them appreciating what they'd learned and making space—physical and psychological—for new learning.

At some point, I stopped making paper copies and instead posted course materials online for students to access on their devices. Their drives became a jumble of readings, graphic organizers, freewrites, notes, and writing projects—and that was just for English class. We needed an online version of the unit clear-out, so I had students create a "useful materials" folder for anything they wanted to save. Instead of having me tell them what to keep, they had to ask themselves and one another what they might want to access easily during future units, in my class or in other classes, this year or afterward. The unit clear-out was not just materials management; it invited collaborative critical thinking about how their materials had been and could continue to be useful.

Their writing went into a different folder. Perhaps they'd created this work to fulfill an assignment, but now the writing was *theirs*. Thus, the unit clear-out became an act of space-making, appreciating their learning, and claiming their authorship.

Onward

This chapter was about orienting rituals that help students transition into, within, and out of a unit. Just as orientation programs help new students find their way around the school building, orienting rituals help all students find their way around their learning so they can fully engage in it. The next chapter is about how to offer students a choice in how they learn and help them choose learning tasks they find meaningful.

4

Values-Based Task Choice

There I was, new to the school where I taught 7th grade English, trying to plan a poetry unit, when I found out most of my students *hated* poetry. One of them summed up the problem: "Every poem we have to read for school is either boring or it makes no sense, and if it does make sense and it isn't boring, then we have to talk about it until it becomes boring, and then we have to write a boring essay about it."

Clearly, my students needed new ways to interact with poetry. If they didn't find poetry inherently interesting, then they needed ways to bring their interests to it. If the traditional response task—an essay—felt stale, they needed ways to respond that would feel exciting and personal yet also helped them practice their critical reading and analytical writing skills. With those goals in mind, I developed a set of poetry response tasks from which students could choose. Each task included an analytical writing component, but analytical writing doesn't have to be an essay; it can take many forms and occur in conjunction with other types of responding.

The assignment choices included making an anthology of poems on a similar theme, choreographing a dance based on a poem, recording a remix of a poem, and designing a BuzzFeed-style "which poem are you" quiz. I had a grand old time doing each assignment so my students would be able to visualize the end project. I made a four-course dinner menu based on Rita Dove's "Flash Cards," a remix of "Sadie and Maud" by Gwendolyn Brooks, and a "Which Mari Evans Poem Are You?" quiz that I actually posted online for my friends to take (although I'm pretty sure I'm the only person who took it).

As much as I enjoyed doing my own assignments, the greater joy came from seeing how students approached them. Claudia's slideshow of the Langston Hughes poem "I, Too" included her sketches of the poet and of various civil rights leaders, and it ended with Barack Obama, who at the time had just been elected. After learning about metaphor during the unit, Jesse realized he used metaphors to communicate his feelings to his therapist, so he created an anthology of poems that use metaphors to communicate emotions that are hard to express directly. Teddy, who struggled to express anything in writing, wrote a beautiful and heartfelt essay explaining how three poems about running expressed things he learned from his track coach.

Although I provided nine different options, I also invited students to invent their own poetry response task that involved critical reading, creative interpreting, and analytical writing. Felix baked a cake inspired by Edgar Allan Poe's "Annabel Lee." Each layer's color and flavor represented some aspect of a corresponding stanza in the poem. Hannah sketched a fashion collection inspired by Shakespearean sonnets. Joy created mixed-media art based on a Richard Wright haiku about white snowflakes on a Black boy's hands. She photographed her own hands, printed two copies, painted one black and the other white, and pasted the two images on a canvas she'd painted black and white. Then she cut out black and white circles and pasted them to the canvas to resemble black and white snow falling on her hands. Joy's artwork paid homage to Wright's poem while also exploring her own multiracial identity.

When we offer students a menu of learning tasks—or when we help them invent their own—students can choose the tasks through which they can learn the content, use their strengths, express their ideas, and discover their values. However, the truth is that when students can choose a learning task, they sometimes do whatever feels easy, familiar, or comfortable—as opposed to doing what truly matters to them. This chapter is about how to design diverse, meaningful learning tasks from which students can choose and how to help students make choices that effectively serve their interests, needs, and values.

Generating Potential Task Choices

A unit—a timebound study of a particular topic—consists of tasks that build on one another and move toward a learning outcome. Learning tasks might include

- Watching a video.
- Solving a series of problems.
- Writing a diary entry.
- Interviewing a relative.
- Reading a picture book.
- Building a model.
- Creating a movement sequence.

These are generic learning tasks that apply to a wide range of units. For example, students might watch a video of a particular scene in *Hamlet* or one that demonstrates how to add fractions.

Notice that a task is what *students* do in order to learn the content, whereas a lesson is what the *teacher* creates to facilitate that learning. A single lesson might include multiple tasks; for example, students might watch a video about how to add fractions, solve a series of fraction addition problems, and then write diary entries about how they solved the problems—all in the same class period. Conversely, one learning task might span several class periods; students might spend two days choreographing movement sequences to portray tectonic plate interactions. Finally, some learning tasks occur outside the classroom, in which case we call them field trips, homework, or asynchronous learning. These terms refer to where, when, and with whom the task occurs, as opposed to what kind of task it is.

Because there are so many different ways to learn about almost any topic, you can present students with a variety of tasks from which they can

FIGURE 4.1

Example Task Brainstorm

Things My Students Could Do to Learn About

PLANT GROWTH

1. Look at and describe germinating seeds under a microscope.
2. Read and summarize an article about how different kinds of plants grow.
3. Graph plant heights as a function of how much light they received.
4. Narrate a time lapse video of a growing plant.
5. Interview a local gardener about how they help plants grow.
6. Draw a plant every day in an observation journal and label evidence of its growth.
7. Choreograph a movement sequence to represent stages of plant growth.
8. Write a comparative review of two picture books about plant growth.
9. Visit the local botanical gardens and make a list of things you learned about plant growth.
10. Make trading cards of biotic and abiotic factors that influence plant growth.
11. Create a simple board game that teaches young children about plant growth.
12. Write a story from the perspective of a growing plant.

choose. To think of potential learning tasks for one of your units, try this exercise:

1. Jot down the topic of a unit you teach.
2. Above where you wrote your unit topic, write "Things My Students Could Do to Learn About" (see Figure 4.1).
3. List at least 10 potential learning tasks for that unit. If you've been teaching this topic for a while, you already use various learning tasks as part of your unit, but this is an opportunity to imagine new possibilities.

Figure 4.1 shows a task brainstorm for a unit on plant growth. Use its list of learning tasks to help you, not limit you.

Task Variety

Giving choice could be as simple as telling students they can solve any five fraction problems from a set of ten or letting them decide whether to hand-write or type their paragraphs about seed germination. However, these options are fundamentally very similar. When students have a wider variety of tasks from which to choose, they're more likely to find ways of learning that fit their interests, strengths, and needs.

In creating a variety of learning tasks, you might find it helpful to distinguish between *receptive* and *expressive* learning tasks. In a receptive learning task, students take in information about a topic—whether by experiencing something for themselves, asking others, or reading a text. In an expressive learning task, students use something they're learning to create work of their own. That work can take many different forms, including data display charts and graphs, written compositions in any format or genre, visual artwork, performance, and interactive objects.

When students engage in a receptive learning task, we often ask them to record what they see or hear, such as by annotating a text or filling out a graphic organizer, and to interpret its meaning in a paragraph or discussion. When students engage in an expressive learning task, we often ask them to explain what they've created, such as by writing an artist statement or making introductory remarks.

Figure 4.2 offers examples of receptive and expressive learning tasks. When we offer a variety of receptive learning tasks, students can choose how they take in information. When we offer a variety of expressive learning tasks, students can choose the type of work they create.

Choice Boards

One way to offer students a wide variety of learning tasks is to use a choice board. Choice boards contain various tasks that move students toward the same overall learning outcome. Many choice boards come as three-by-three grids with nine choices, although they can take any shape and include any number of tasks. Figure 4.3 shows a choice board I used for my 7th grade poetry unit. Each task is a different way to interact with poetry, but they all involve critical reading, creative interpretation, and analytical writing.

Teachers use choice boards in various ways. Some teachers ask their students to select just one task through which they will learn the content. Other teachers ask their students to select any three tasks in a row—across, down,

FIGURE 4.2

Receptive and Expressive Learning Tasks

Receptive Learning Tasks		
Direct Experience	Observation	Examination of artifacts
	Experiments	Games
	Field studies	Free play
Asking Others	Interviews	Focus groups
	Community surveys	Storytelling sessions
Reading a Text	*Verbal*	*Visual*
	Articles	Paintings
	Essays	Photographs
	Case studies	Diagrams
	Websites	Charts
	Novels	Infographics
	Poems	Comics
	Auditory	*Audiovisual*
	Talks	Films
	Podcasts	Videos
	Songs	Television shows
	Archived interviews	Advertisements
	Spoken word	Animations

Expressive Learning Tasks		
Data display charts	Table	Map
	Graph	Infographic
	Diagram	Word cloud
Written compositions	Essay (personal, analytical)	Letter
	Report	Résumé
	Article	Recipe
	Blog	Menu
	Vignette	Budget
	Poem	Brochure
	Journal	Business plan
Visual artworks	Sketch	Photo essay
	Painting	Slideshow
	Collage	Comic
Performances	Demonstration	Concert
	Dramatization	Spoken word
	Dance	Recitation
Interactive objects	Board game	Trading cards
	Puzzle	Toy
	Quiz	Food

Source: Copyright 2023 by Lauren Porosoff.

FIGURE 4.3
Example Choice Board

Mini-Anthology	**Tribute**	**Collage**
Choose a poem with a message you feel strongly about. Find eight more poems with the same topic or theme and write one of your own. Write an introduction that explains what the 10 poems have in common and why you've put them in a particular order.	Choose three poems for a particular person. Write a letter to the person explaining why you chose each poem for them, quoting specific lines. Assemble the poems and letter into a collection you can imagine giving to the person. (Whether you actually give it to them is up to you.)	Find 12 images from different poems that fit a particular category. Make a collage that includes the lines of poetry as well as pictures you draw or find. Write an artist statement explaining where the images come from, how they go together, and why the topic matters to you.
Dramatization	**Dance**	**Slideshow**
Choose a poem that tells a story. Annotate the text with stage directions. Include notes about movement, the use of any props, and when to pause. Perform and record the skit, introduced with an explanation of your directorial choices.	Choose a poem with lots of action. Annotate the text with movements for each line. Write an introduction explaining what emotions and ideas the movements convey. Perform the dance yourself, or direct someone else in a performance.	Choose a poem with vivid imagery. Make drawings or take photos to portray each part of your poem. Insert each picture into a slide that also includes the relevant lines of poetry and an explanation of how the picture connects to the poem.
Remix	**Dinner Menu**	**"What Poem are You?" Quiz**
Choose a poem with strong rhythm and rhyme. Record a remix that repeats and resequences parts and includes lines from other poems or songs. Add effects or music. Write production notes explaining how your remix expands on the poem's meaning.	Choose a longer poem. Think of dishes that reflect the poem's themes and imagery. Create a multicourse dinner menu with dishes that pair with each of the poem's parts. Include descriptions of each dish and explanations of how the dish goes with a particular part of the poem.	Find five poems by one poet. Match each poem to a personality. Write questions about the user's personality, with multiple choice answers corresponding to each poem. Then write descriptions of how each poem reflects a particular personality, which will become the quiz results.

Source: Copyright 2023 by Lauren Porosoff.

or diagonal, like in tic-tac-toe—which become their learning tasks for the unit. Still other teachers assign a point value to each learning task, usually based on the task's complexity or labor requirement, and ask students to do any combination of tasks that garners some number of points. Figure 4.4 shows a choice board for a unit on plant growth, with point values assigned to each learning task. Students could select any combination of tasks as long as they do at least, say, 10 points' worth of work.

FIGURE 4.4

Example Choice Board with Point Values

Look at and describe germinating seeds under a microscope. +2	Read and summarize an article about how different kinds of plants grow. +3	Graph plant heights as a function of how much light they received. +3
Interview a local gardener about how they help plants grow. +5	Draw a plant every day in an observation journal and label evidence of its growth. +4	Write a comparative review of two picture books about plant growth. +6
Make trading cards of biotic and abiotic factors that influence plant growth. +5	Create a simple board game that teaches young children about plant growth. +7	Write a story from the perspective of a growing plant. +6

Source: Copyright 2023 by Lauren Porosoff.

Some teachers use labor-based grading contracts, an equity practice developed by writing professor Asao Inoue (2019). For a labor-based choice board, the teacher specifies what it means to complete each task—how much time students need to spend on it and what they need to produce. Students then negotiate how many tasks they'd have to do to get a *B* for the unit (perhaps three) and how many additional tasks they'd have to do to get an *A* (perhaps two more). Instead of evaluating the work product's quality, which according to Inoue would reflect dominant cultural standards and thus reproduce oppression, the teacher simply records whether the student completed the task. The only way a student would *not* get a *B* is if they didn't complete enough tasks. Thus, in a labor-based choice board, students choose their learning tasks *and* their grade for the unit.

Finally, some teachers leave a blank space on the choice board that students can fill in with learning tasks they invent themselves. For example, my younger child loves to play with LEGO bricks, so he might create his own learning task where he builds the stages of plant growth out of LEGO. My older child loves to draw and also loves geography, so they might draw how plants grow in different global regions.

A student-created learning task becomes part of whatever system the teacher uses for the overall choice board. It could be the one task the student who created it selects. It could be part of a "tic-tac-toe" series of three activities. The teacher and student could agree on a number of points the task is worth. It could figure into a labor-based grading contract in which students who complete some number of teacher-designed tasks get a *B* but those who create and complete their own tasks get an *A*.

Giving students an opportunity to create their own tasks adds work for you because you'll have to make sure the tasks they create fulfill the unit's learning objectives, but you're also providing more ways students can bring their interests, strengths, and values to their learning.

Looking Critically at #VoiceAndChoice

Students have agency over their learning when they can choose tasks that best match their interests, strengths, needs, and values. If students can invent their own learning tasks, then they have not only a choice in how they learn but also a voice. Voice and choice! It sounds exhilarating. It even rhymes. No wonder so many teachers love choice boards, and #VoiceAndChoice has become a shorthand for empowering students.

Sometimes, though, what looks like choice . . . isn't. My area has dozens of afterschool and summer programs for kids, but almost none have staff with the special needs training it would take for my son to attend. Clothing stores carry outfits in many different sizes and styles, but my older child struggles to find ones appropriate for nonbinary kids like them. A meaningful choice requires having access to multiple options that will work for that individual.

If we give students a choice of learning tasks, then we need to make sure they *all* have access to *all* the options. Even the choice to handwrite or type is meaningless for students who lack access to a device. However, access to supplies is not the only factor that limits meaningful choice. Take the plant growth choice board in Figure 4.4; some families might have a living room full of board games that could serve as models for a plant growth game, whereas other families don't have a living room, let alone board games. Some students might want to interview a local gardener but do not know where or how to find one. Creating equity means we must provide sufficient time, supplies, models, and support for every student to have access to every task.

This doesn't mean every task must be equally easy for every student. The observation journal task might be easier for a student who regularly draws and takes art classes than for a student who doesn't (although not necessarily; the student with an art background might spend much more time on the drawing task or might not have a background in scientific drawing). However, we should not assume that a student who "isn't artsy" or has dysgraphia *couldn't* choose the drawing task or that only students who already like art *would* choose it.

Even when people have a meaningful choice, they don't always choose to do what serves their needs. Think about it. Do you always eat the healthiest food available? Go to bed early enough to get a good night's sleep? Exercise? Fold your laundry? Floss? Given choice, people often choose whatever feels easy, convenient, familiar, comfortable, or fun in the short term—but not necessarily what will most effectively help them achieve their long-term goals (Waltz & Follette, 2009).

Maybe you've seen "adulting" stickers that say things like, "I didn't hit the snooze button today" or "I paid most of my bills on time." The term *adulting* implies that it takes a certain amount of maturity to do things that aren't fun in the moment but that help us in the long term. If adults don't always choose what's most effective in the long term, we have no reason to think children will, either.

Students have another reason not to choose tasks that will be meaningful to them. Many (if not most) schools assign rankings to students, whether with grades, honors distinctions, badges, points, or a fantasy status such as *biome boss* or *ecology emperor*. We might tell students they have a choice among learning tasks and actively discourage them from choosing based on how they think the task will affect their position in the academic hierarchy, but if we rank them, many students will choose to do whatever they think will help them achieve the highest possible ranking—regardless of how meaningful it is to them. Other students find schoolwork so aversive that they'll choose whichever task seems like it will be the fastest one to get through.

Knowing all this, many teachers encourage students to do certain tasks based on what they, the teacher, think would be best in the long term.

That might help students learn, but then they are not really making a choice anymore.

Fostering Values-Based Task Selection

If we want our students to make choices but know they won't always choose what's most effective for them in the long term, we can help them evaluate their options more carefully. The following task selection protocol helps students identify potential reasons for choosing a task, articulate for themselves why they're making a particular choice, and hear their peers' reasons for making choices—all so they choose more effectively. Use this protocol when students are choosing learning tasks that will require significant time and labor or when the resulting learning has especially high stakes.

Task Selection Protocol

1. Give students a menu or choice board that includes several different learning tasks. Ask them to silently read their various options.
2. Invite students to ask clarifying questions about what the tasks entail. A clarifying question will help them understand the task itself—what they need to do, how they might go about doing it, and what the work product will look like.
3. Ask students to mark the task that sounds most *appealing* at that moment. Appeal depends on what students tend to enjoy, what they're thinking about and feeling that day, and what's happening in their environment (such as whether they have friends in the class or what materials are available).
4. Ask students to mark the task that sounds most *useful* in helping them understand the unit topic or develop a relevant skill. Whereas appeal depends on how students feel while doing the task, usefulness depends on its result. Asking about usefulness helps students notice that what's meaningful in the long term isn't always what's fun or comfortable in the short term.
5. Ask students to mark the task that sounds most *different* from what they usually do as learners or in their lives. When asked to notice

which task would be different, students compare potential future experiences with their past experiences. Even if a task sounds challenging or weird, students might become curious about it and more willing to try it if they explicitly identify it as unlike what they've done in the past.

6. Ask students to write what they'll do and why, using the sentence frame *I will* ___ *because* ___. They fill in the first blank with one of the three tasks they just marked and the second blank with one or more reasons they're choosing that task.

> For example, a student might write
>
> — "I will make trading cards of biotic and abiotic factors that influence plant growth because I have trading cards at home, but I've never actually made them before."
>
> — "I will write a comparative review of picture books because picture books explain things really clearly, and that would really help me understand how plants grow."
>
> — "I will choreograph a dance that shows the stages of plant growth because I like being able to move around instead of sitting at a desk."

Making statements such as these empowers students to hold themselves accountable to their own reasons for choosing a particular task.

7. Have all students share their statements. You could go around the room and have everyone read their statements out loud, or you could have students write their statements on the board (whether it's physical or virtual). No matter how they share, stating their choices and their reasons for making them amounts to a values-based commitment that their classmates can now help them keep.

When students hear their peers' reasons for making certain choices, they might notice more ways they can make their own learning meaningful. Imagine that a student says, "I will interview a local gardener about how they help plants grow because I don't usually get to learn stuff for school by talking to people who do those things in real life." Another student hears that statement and realizes that he, too, rarely gets to learn from community experts but would like to. Even if that second student doesn't interview a gardener during the plant growth unit, he's now more aware of why he might find it meaningful to learn from local experts, and he might look for opportunities to do so in the future.

As your students share, you can quickly assess their choices and provide support as needed. For example, after all students share their plant growth task choices, you could ask everyone who's interviewing a local gardener to gather so they can discuss how to find someone to interview, set up a time, and prepare good questions. If certain students choose a task you think they'll struggle to complete, you can head over to them as soon as everyone starts working, make sure they understand the task, and check in regularly to help them through any difficulties.

By contrast, if a student chooses a task you think is too easy for them, you can let them know you think they're capable of excelling at a more challenging task, and then ask how the task they chose will challenge them—or how they might make it challenging. The conversation might get the student to pick a different option or add complexity to the one they chose. It's also possible that you will realize the task is more difficult than you'd thought or that the student is deliberately choosing an easier task because they have a lot going on in their life. Even if the student sticks with an "easy" task just because they feel like it, they now know that you see them as a strong student and that you care about them enough to push them toward meeting their potential.

Some students might not take task selection seriously. They'll say things like, "I will read the article about how plants grow because I enjoy being bored" or "I will graph plant heights because that's what Jessica picked" or "I will write a story from the perspective of a growing plant because I *am* a growing plant." Depending on what the student says and how disruptive it is, you might address the comment in the moment or just continue the share-out and at a later point find a way to give that student the attention and connection they're seeking.

Other students will be dishonest about their choices. For example, a student might say, "I will look at seeds under a microscope because I'm interested in seeing things from a different perspective" when in fact they just think looking under a microscope will be the fastest task to complete.

They usually know why they're choosing a task even if they don't say the real reason out loud, and calling them out will most likely just evoke defensiveness or more dishonesty. You're better off saying nothing and then having students assess the results of their choices.

Fostering Values-Based Choice Assessment

Selection protocols help students consider their choices but don't guarantee they'll choose effectively. Even a student who makes a well-reasoned choice might find their experience doesn't match their expectations or that their work product is disappointing in some way. Students who *do* make effective choices but don't understand *why* might not make similarly effective choices in the future.

The questions in Figure 4.5 help students assess how their choice of task worked out for them, based on what they think is important. Process questions help students notice how they felt as they worked and discover whether their task choice led to the sort of experience they wanted. Outcome questions help students assess the extent to which their work was worthwhile, regardless of how they felt while working. Finally, planning questions help students make choices in the future that work just as well, if not better, for them.

Students can respond in writing so they have a record of their thinking and then share their responses with a partner, in a small group, or in a whole-class discussion. If you frequently give students a choice among learning tasks, having them assess the impacts of their choices each time helps them become more skillful choosers.

Noticing how their choices worked out for them won't guarantee that they'll make effective choices in the future, but it helps them build the capacity to judge their choices based on their own experiences—rather than relying on *your* judgment.

That said, students will likely respond differently depending on whether they reflect before or after you evaluate their work. If they already know they got a high grade, they might express more satisfaction with their choices, thus substituting your judgment for their own. Students who tend toward

FIGURE 4.5

Choice Assessment Question Bank

Process Questions *(Give one or two.)*

- How much did you enjoy this task? Rate it on a scale of 1 (not at all enjoyable) to 10 (extremely enjoyable). If some parts were more enjoyable than others, write the parts and give them different ratings.
- How challenging was the task? Rate it on a scale of 1 (not at all challenging) to 10 (extremely challenging). Are you satisfied with that level of challenge, or do you think you needed more or less? Why?
- Which parts of the task did you spend the most time on? Which parts did you spend the least time on? How satisfied are you with the way you allocated your work time?
- How much time did you spend on the task as a whole? Are you glad you put in that amount of time, or do you wish you'd put in more or less? What would that have accomplished?
- Were there any unexpected parts of the process? This could be anything you realized or discovered as you worked.

Outcome Questions *(Give one or two.)*

- How satisfied are you with the end product? Rate it on a scale of 1 (not at all satisfied) to 10 (extremely satisfied). If you're more satisfied with some parts than others, note down the parts and give them different ratings.
- What did you learn about the topic from doing this task? How satisfied are you with your learning? Rate it on a scale of 1 (not at all satisfied) to 10 (extremely satisfied).
- What *else* did you learn as a result of doing this task? These might be other topics you learned about or things you learned how to do. When can you imagine that knowledge coming in handy?
- What (if anything) did you learn about yourself from doing this task?

Planning Questions *(Give one.)*

- Next time you have a learning task similar to the one you chose, how will you approach it? What will you do similarly and differently?
- Next time you have a choice of learning tasks, how will you make that choice?

self-criticism might evaluate outcomes more harshly if their grades are lower than they expected, and students who tend toward self-defensiveness might evaluate their choices more generously—as if to prove they were right and you were wrong.

If students assess their choices *before* receiving your evaluation of their work, they can only measure their satisfaction in terms of their own values. A student might have learned a lot about plant growth from the process of making an observation journal, even if she wasn't able to communicate that understanding in the journal itself. She might also be satisfied with how persistently she observed the plant and how artistically she crafted the journal.

Although persistence and artistry might not be assessed in science class, they might be important values for that student. When doing future work, she might look for ways to be persistent and artistic while also meeting the teacher's standards.

Self-assessment gives students a chance to consider how they've brought their own values to their work before considering how well they've lived up to someone else's standards. If they're disappointed after seeing your feedback (and their grade), they have another opportunity to consider how their choices influenced their work product and different choices they might make next time.

If you invite students to share their self-assessments, you'll get to learn more about what makes work interesting, challenging, and meaningful for your students, which might help you as you design future learning tasks. Regardless of how you use the information, though, your students need opportunities to assess past choices so they can make more effective choices in the future.

Limitations of Giving Students a Choice of Learning Tasks

Even if we make all possible choices accessible, and even if we use selection and assessment tools to help students make values-based choices, asking students to choose their own learning tasks has other limitations that are harder to overcome. First, if students can do any set of learning tasks in any order, then the tasks won't necessarily build on one another. After doing several tasks from the plant growth choice board, students might feel like they've done a bunch of cool activities, but they won't necessarily feel like those activities coalesce into a single meaningful learning experience or that each task draws on skills and knowledge they developed from doing the previous task. Even if students feel satisfied after completing the tasks they chose, they might derive even more satisfaction from reaching a larger understanding as a result of doing interconnected tasks that you have thoughtfully sequenced.

Second, if students can choose their own sets of learning tasks, there is no single shared experience. Students then miss an opportunity to build trust, interdependence, and solidarity in the process of doing meaningful work together. Providing choice fosters a sense of connection *to the content* because students get to use their strengths and do what's interesting and important to them. However, task choice can hinder students' sense of connection *to each other* if they're all doing separate activities. We should create opportunities for students to choose learning tasks based on their values, but use these opportunities judiciously when designing units.

Onward

This chapter was about offering students a choice of learning tasks and helping them make effective choices based on their values—all so they feel more connected to the content. In the next chapter, we'll move from how students can connect *to the content* they're learning to how they can connect *to the work* they do. We'll see how student work can affirm their identities, leverage their values, and provide opportunities for them to be and become who they are.

PART

II

• • •

Engaging with Their Work

5

Affirming Assignments

In her essay "A Mother's Work," ecologist Robin Wall Kimmerer (2013) describes her efforts to make the pond near her house swimmable for her daughters. She rakes up algae and turns it into compost, gathers mint for her tea from the pond's banks, cuts back nearby willows to help them grow, and makes garden trellises from the branches. She tries not to disturb birds that nest in the willows and returns tadpoles to the water when they come up with the algae. She says of the pond, "Our lives became intertwined in ways both material and spiritual. It's been a balanced exchange: I worked on the pond and the pond worked on me, and together we made a good home" (p. 95).

Although her daughters grow up before Kimmerer can make the pond safe to swim in, she reflects on what she did accomplish through her work: "[T]he pond has shown me that being a good mother doesn't end with creating a home where just my children can flourish. . . . There are grandchildren to nurture, and frog children, nestlings, goslings, seedlings, and spores, and I still want to be a good mother" (p. 97).

Mucking out a pond is cold, wet, and icky work, yet for Kimmerer, it was deeply worthwhile. Her work

- Had *real-world benefits.* Her daughters enjoyed having campfires and picnics by the pond's edge even though they didn't get to swim in it, she got usable goods for her home and garden, countless living beings thrived in the cleaner water, and the ecosystem was restored.
- Was an act of *self-expression.* Through it, she communicated love for her daughters, the land, and its inhabitants.
- Was an act of *self-making.* By doing it, she became the person she wanted to be.

When students describe their psychological experience of schoolwork—how they feel while they're working, what motivates them to work, and what they think of the finished product or performance—they don't exactly sound like a Robin Wall Kimmerer essay. Faced with an assignment, students often express anxiety, dread, resentment, or exhausted resignation about having to complete it. Sometimes their only motivation to do the work is to avoid getting in trouble for *not* doing it, or they comply because they don't see themselves as having a choice.

Often, students put forth effort because they want to do well; if they get grades, scores, badges, or any other symbol of achievement, they want to get the highest one possible. However, that recognition and any happy feelings that come along with it don't occur until *after* the student has finished the work, and only *if* they attain the status they wanted. The act of working doesn't necessarily feel fulfilling, and the finished product or performance doesn't necessarily mean anything to them; it's merely how they got their reward.

Schoolwork does not have to be this way. From a teacher's perspective, schoolwork results in a product or performance that provides evidence of a student's knowledge and skills. However, from the student's perspective, the act of doing schoolwork can be joyful, fulfilling, and even liberating because liberation doesn't mean freedom from work; it means the freedom to do work that matters and to approach it in a way that brings vitality and satisfaction. That process begins when the work itself feels both important and affirming.

This chapter is about how teachers can design assignments that transform students' psychological experience of schoolwork. First, we'll explore three features of affirming work: it makes a contribution to the real world, expresses what matters to students, and helps them become the people they want to be. We'll then discover how to write assignments that lead to affirming work.

Schoolwork as a Real-World Contribution

Students feel like their work matters when its outcome has an impact beyond the classroom. For example, many music and dance classes culminate in concerts to which students invite family members and friends. Most people who attend school concerts are there to support their loved ones, but there is at least the potential for the audience to be entertained, educated, and inspired. Another example of schoolwork mattering beyond the classroom is human-centered design. Students interview community members to learn what problems they encounter so they can propose, build, and install solutions. These products and performances provide the teacher with a basis of assessment *and also* have a real-world impact.

In arts and engineering classes, students already create performances and products, but what about traditional academic disciplines such as English, history, science, math, and language? How can work in those classes have a real-world impact?

Unlike the *project-driven* units in arts and engineering classes, many units in traditional academic classes are *inquiry-driven*. During inquiry-driven units, students explore a topic and strive to understand it more fully. Inquiries are integrative; each learning task contributes to a broader or deeper understanding of the topic.

A good way to assess students at the end of an inquiry is to have them use their broader and deeper understandings to make something that has a real-world benefit. For example, students who've explored how fractions enable fair sharing could make chore charts that show how their families can fairly share the housework according to the number of minutes each chore takes. Students who've explored chromosomes could make karyotypes and write explainers about what they tell and don't tell about a person. These projects have the potential to make an impact on others.

Although most units include some inquiry, not all are inquiry-driven. During *rehearsal-driven* units, students develop a meaningful skill set through practice. Rehearsal-driven units are cumulative; each learning task maintains and increases students' repertoire of skills. Practice might not make perfect, but rehearsal makes reliable.

Rehearsing skills in a relatively low-stakes context enables students to reliably use them when the stakes are higher, but if the stakes are too low, students won't feel like rehearsal matters. Students need something meaningful to rehearse *for*—a performance during which they use the skills they've learned. For example, students who have practiced measuring solids and liquids could put their skills to use in helping to build and care for a school garden. Students who have practiced evaluating media for bias could create PSAs for their peers about popular YouTube channels. Again, these projects have the potential to make a positive impact beyond the classroom.

Although we might assign work so we can assess students' knowledge and skills, the resulting product or performance can benefit the community. Figure 5.1 includes various potential benefits of student-made work that can also serve as assessment evidence.

Even when student work serves as assessment evidence *and* has a potential impact beyond the classroom, a *potential* impact means students won't know whether and how their work made a difference in the world until after they've finished working. For example, a student who designs a meme about lab safety won't know whether her peers find it entertaining until after she finishes making it. A student who writes an article about an elder's experiences during the Cold War era won't know whether it inspires action until after he completes the interview, writes the article, shares it with others, and watches what they do. That's quite a lot of work without any guarantee that the desired outcome will happen.

Psychologists Matthieu Villatte, Jennifer Villatte, and Steven Hayes (2016) identify two fundamentally different types of intrinsic motivation: conditional and hierarchical. If we frame an action only as a *condition*

FIGURE 5.1

Real-World Benefits of Student-Made Products and Performances

Community Benefit	Example Assignment	Skill/Knowledge Assessed
Informing people	Record a PSA for middle and high school students that reveals one or more types of bias on a popular YouTube channel.	Critically analyzing media for bias (history, English, civics)
Entertaining people	Design a meme that encourages safe behavior in the lab.	Using lab safety procedures (science)
Inspiring thought	Using the work of Zanele Muholi as a model, create a self-portrait that challenges stereotypes about one or more of your sociocultural identifiers.	How is a self-portrait different from a selfie? (visual art)
Inspiring action	After interviewing an elder about their experiences during the Cold War, write an article about how the elder's experiences should inform our actions today.	How did different people experience the Cold War differently? How can Cold War–thinking and actions inform our thinking and actions today? (history)
Solving a local problem	Make a family chore chart that fairly shares the time and labor of caring for your home.	How can fractions help us share fairly? (math)
Preserving a local asset	Using essays by Anna Winger and Michael Twitty as models, write an essay about a memorable experience with food. Accompany your essay with a related recipe.	Supporting a thesis, using imagery, transitioning from one idea to another (English)
Caring for others	Create a how-to video, narrated and captioned in Spanish, showing how to prepare a favorite healthy snack.	Using command-form verbs, using food vocabulary (Spanish)
Caring for oneself	Design a wellness plan for yourself that includes nourishment, physical exercise, social connection, play, and rest. Explain how your wellness plan will help you feel beautiful.	How can girls and women resist sexism and redefine *beautiful* for themselves? (physical education, health)

under which an outcome will occur ("If I write this article, readers will be inspired to fight for civil rights"), we won't feel satisfaction unless and until that outcome occurs. However, if we also frame the action as *part of* living by our values ("Writing this article is an opportunity for me to treat my elders lovingly"), we find satisfaction in the process of doing the action itself. We might feel disappointed if the work doesn't have the impact we hoped for, but enacting our values affirms who we are even when we don't get the outcome we wanted.

Schoolwork as Self-Expression

Donovan Livingston is an educator and poet who attended Harvard Graduate School of Education, and when he finished the program, he was invited to be the student speaker at convocation. The speech went viral. It consisted mostly of a poem Livingston (2016) wrote about his experiences as a student that motivated his eventual work as an educator. He says he was called "disruptive" and "talkative" until his 7th grade teacher "introduced [him] to the sound of [his] own voice." He calls on his fellow educators to see the "celestial potential" in every student and "inspire galaxies of greatness" in our classrooms.

To get a sense of what Livingston means by "celestial potential," think of someone who's widely considered to be a genius. Now imagine a younger version of that person in your class. If you happen to teach physics, you might get excited (and perhaps a bit intimidated) at the thought of Albert Einstein as your student. Even if you teach another subject, though, wouldn't you be curious to see what Einstein would do in your class?

I'd love to read 7th grade Einstein's vignette collection. I'd love to see how the 7th grade versions of Cesar Chavez and Dolores Huerta, who cofounded the National Farm Workers Association and were civil rights leaders, would use imagery in their neighborhood essays. Mae Jemison *literally* had celestial potential. After getting her degree in chemical engineering, she became a physician, then became the first Black woman astronaut—all before her 35th birthday (Alexander, 2019). I'd love to hear Jemison as a 7th grader, performing the poem she'd write for my spoken-word unit. If people you consider brilliant were in your class, wouldn't you want to see their work, even if it's outside their eventual area of expertise?

As exciting as that thought is, I then imagine the younger versions of these geniuses in class with the less experienced version of me—the one who assigned five-paragraph essays and made students fill out graphic organizers with assertions, supporting statements, quotations, and transitions before they were allowed to do any actual writing. If I collected 65 essays, 45 of them were indistinguishable from one another, eight or nine were fascinating in a good way, another eight or nine were fascinating in a bad way, and the remaining few couldn't even be called essays. Now-me would be embarrassed if then-me had made Einstein, Chavez, Huerta, or Jemison do those old assignments. Actually, now-me *is* embarrassed because then-me had students with celestial potential. You do, too. Don't you want to hear what they have to say?

If we assume students have varying levels of knowledge and skill, we'll give assignments to help us determine who can do excellent work, who can do an adequate job, and who will struggle. However, if we assume everyone in the room has celestial potential, then we might give assignments that encourage students to really express who they are. We might, as Livingston said of his 7th grade teacher, introduce our students to the sound of their own voices and help them use their voices to say something they think is important.

Schoolwork as Selfing

Psychologists Louise McHugh, Ian Stewart, and Priscilla Almada (2019) use the word *self* as a verb. *Selfing* is the ongoing process of discovering and building who we are. As soon as we become conscious of our own existence, "we begin to interpret, explain, evaluate, predict, and rationalize our behavior" and then "strive to organize our descriptions and evaluations of our personal histories and tendencies into a coherent network—a consistent presentation of the self" (p. 106).

For example, Robin Wall Kimmerer (2013) understood herself as "a good mother" (p. 97) after noticing how she cared for her daughters, other creatures, and the land. Each action she took to restore the pond was an act of *selfing*—discovering who she was and wanted to be, and then becoming that person.

According to McHugh, Stewart, and Almada (2019), every conscious experience we have—our "current and historical feelings, sensations, preferences, abilities, thoughts, interactions, and learning" (p. 106)—informs our selfing process. Values play a special role in selfing; we have various experiences, notice which ones make us feel fulfilled, and derive our values accordingly. Those values guide our goals, which guide our actions.

For example, when I was a child, my parents surrounded me with books, took me to museums, and asked me lots of questions about the world. These experiences were tremendously fulfilling, and over time, curiosity became one of my values. That value guided my goal of fostering curiosity in my classroom, which guided many of my actions as a teacher, such as offering stimulating texts, sharing my genuine questions, and encouraging students to ask their own.

As students create various products and performances for school, they make decisions. They might ask themselves, "What topic will I research?" "What colors will I use in this painting?" "How carefully will I follow the steps of the lab procedure?" "How many times will I practice my French presentation?" "Do I want to use the cool font I like, or should I use one that will be easier for people to read?" "How will I make my probability game informative but also fun to play?" "How will I ask questions of my interviewee so I get the information I need for my Cold War article while also showing them respect and compassion?"

Making such decisions, students don't only choose how to complete the assignment. They also discover and develop the values they want to live by. Those values guide our students' goals, which guide their actions, which help them discover their values, and the cycle continues. It might sound grandiose to frame writing an essay or doing a math project as *selfing*, but in a very real way, creating products and performances for school is not only self-expression; it's self-construction.

Once we understand everything students do as selfing, we might start to think differently about the kinds of things we ask students to do. We might wonder how we can design assignments that honor the selves students bring to their work and the selves they will create in the process of working.

Designing an Affirming Assignment

We've now seen that work, including schoolwork, feels affirming when it makes a positive contribution to the world, serves as authentic self-expression, and helps people choose who they want to be. It's up to the students to decide what they'll contribute to the world, which aspects of themselves they'll express, and how their experiences will inform who they are. However, we can design assignments that invite students to do affirming work, which is a way we can affirm our students themelves. Let's look at three key features of an affirming assignment.

Real-World Resemblance

First, we need to signal to students that their work could make a meaningful contribution in the real world. If we ask them to create a product or performance that only exists in classrooms, they'll have trouble believing it will be useful anywhere else. Five-paragraph essays, math problem sets, spelling word sentences, multiple choice tests, fill-in-the-blank worksheets, and many other assignments exist only in schools. Such assignments can help students build skills through repetitive practice, but at some point, they should get to use those skills to create something that matters beyond school.

An affirming assignment asks students to create a product or performance of the sort that exists in the real world. This product or performance *resembles* a real-world product or performance because students can't be expected to have the skills, knowledge, or resources of a real-world practitioner. For example, if students make animations in earth science class to show how tectonic plates interact, their final products won't look like a Pixar movie, but they'll resemble a type of real-world work. Figure 5.2 offers many examples of real-world products and performances.

You might associate certain types of work with certain classes, such as poems with English, murals with art, and experiments with science. When students do work of the type that practitioners in your discipline do, they discover career options they might one day pursue. However, don't let

FIGURE 5.2

Examples of Real-World Products and Performances

Advertisement	Dance	Menu	Puzzle
Animation	Diagram	Mockumentary	Quiz
Article	Diary	Model	Recitation
Awards ceremony	Documentary	Mural	Reenactment
Banquet	Escape room	Museum	Remix
Blackout poetry	Eulogy	Newsletter	Restorative circle
Blog	Experiment	Newspaper	Resumé
Blueprint	Fantasy bracket	Online environment	Review
Board game	Fashion design	Op-ed	Sales pitch
Brochure	Field journal	Painting	Script
Budget	Focus group	Panel discussion	Short story
Business plan	Game	Personal essay	Social media page
Campaign	Graph	Petition	Song
Catalog	Guided tour	Photo essay	Soundtrack
Chart	How-to video	Picture book	Spoken word
Collage	Interactive timeline	Play	Talk
Comic	Interview	Podcast	Toy
Concert	Lesson	Poem	Travel log
Convention	Letter	Poster presentation	Trial/hearing
Crime scene	Map	Proposal	Website

your preexisting associations limit the types of assignments you consider for your students. We might associate murals with art class, but they could also be a great way for students to inspire action on climate change, a topic they might study in a science or geography course.

Other types of work might not obviously relate to any academic course, yet they might be great ways for students to demonstrate what they've learned in class while making their work matter beyond the classroom. We might not associate board games with the work of historians or chemists, but they could be a great way to teach people about the Industrial Revolution or chemical reactions. If you approach the list of real-world products and performances with an open mind, you might come up with interesting assignments that help your students demonstrate their knowledge and make a real-world impact.

When giving assignments that resemble real-world work, teachers might add conditions that don't exist for practitioners and remove conditions that do. For example, a high school lab report might include many of the same sections as a published study (abstract, procedure, data, discussion, and conclusion), but students might have to add a materials section and *not* have to include a literature review. If middle school history students make board games about the Industrial Revolution, they might have to include a certain number of historical facts but *not* include how long the game takes to play or what it costs. These assignments bring students as close as they can to doing real-world work while still honoring their needs as learners.

An Available Audience

Even if students create a product or performance of the type that exists in the real world, they won't feel like it will make an actual difference unless they have an audience who will use or experience it.

If students make something for self-care purposes—such as a wellness plan, sensory toy, or vision board—then their audience is themselves. However, they might forget to follow the wellness plan, take a sensory break, look at their vision boards, or otherwise interact with whatever they've made. To remedy this, they could set alerts on their phones, email their caregivers to remind them at home, put stickers in their planners, or otherwise signal to themselves that they've made something useful and to use it.

Further, even if the thing they've created is just for themselves, students will need an opportunity to share the experience of using it. To start that discussion, ask students whether they've used the thing: "Have you tried your wellness routine?" "Did you hang up your vision board?" "Have you played with your sensory toy yet?" Ask a few students who did use the thing to say how it felt so they can amplify their sense of success by sharing it with others. Then ask a few students who didn't use theirs to say what got in the way, and invite other students to suggest how they could overcome those obstacles.

Most student-made products and performances have a potential benefit for other people. In those cases, part of creating the assignment will be finding an audience. You could simply have your students read each other's essays or listen to each other's podcasts, or you could invite another class to play your students' board games. However, don't be afraid to imagine wider audiences. If students write reports advocating for more aggressive antipollution laws, they could present their reports to local legislators or send them to voters. If students make Spanish-language how-to videos about making healthy snacks, they could post the videos online, create a social media hashtag for the project, and ask community members to post photos of themselves with the snacks. The more students see their work having an actual impact, the more affirming that work is likely to be.

Remember, though, that your students' work fulfills an assignment you gave, which means they don't have much of a choice as to whether they complete it. They should have a choice as to whether they share it with anyone beyond you and whether it's used for any purpose beyond assessment.

Choosing to share can help students build relationships with others, but choosing *not* to share can help them maintain personal boundaries. This is especially true when students explore topics of personal significance. I've had LGBTQ+ students come out to me through essays they've written for my class. I've read comics about racist microaggressions and poems about grief. I've listened to spoken-word performances about sexual assault. Maybe students are more likely to self-disclose in English and art classes where they tell their own stories, but what they reveal depends more on the assignment, the student, and their relationship with the teacher than the subject.

Even if the topic isn't personal, students might not feel safe sharing their work products, and forcing them to share before they're ready doesn't make them any safer. Students retain agency over their own work when sharing it is optional.

Relatability for Diverse Students

An affirming assignment will be specific enough that every student understands what it entails yet broad enough that every student in a diverse group finds personally meaningful ways to approach it.

Imagine, for example, that an art class has just studied Vincent van Gogh's famous painting *The Starry Night*, which represents a fantasy version of the night sky the artist saw from his window. If asked to paint their own fantasy versions of the night sky, some students might find personally meaningful approaches to the assignment, but others might not care about night skies (and end up just copying van Gogh). If asked to paint a fantasy version of *anything*, some students might identify something meaningful to reinterpret from a fantasy perspective, but others might have no idea what to paint (and perhaps go with a night sky, thus copying van Gogh). However, if asked to take a photo from their window and then paint a fantasy version of that view, every student has a personal connection. It's *their* window from which they see *their* neighborhood. If a student thinks of a different way to relate personally to the assignment—"I spend a lot of time at my grandparents' house, so can I do the window there?"—that works, too.

We've now seen three features of an affirming assignment: it asks students to create something that resembles a real-world product or performance, offers an audience with whom students can choose to share their work, and is broad yet specific enough that all students in a diverse group will find it accessible and relatable. How do we get ideas for assignments that have these features?

Coming Up with Affirming Assignments

If we're looking to assess our students—that is, to determine what they know and can do—they can provide evidence of their knowledge and skills in many different ways. That leaves us room to design assignments whereby students produce assessment evidence *and* experience vitality from doing work they find meaningful. Nevertheless, we might hesitate to let go of existing assignments if they have *some* benefit.

Educator Bob Eberle (1972, 2008) created a method for generating new ideas from old ones, which he calls SCAMPER. Although Eberle's work focuses on student creativity, his method can help teachers generate new assignment ideas.

Figure 5.3 shows the SCAMPER elements as applied to assignment design, along with example brainstorms that came from using SCAMPER on three different assignments. The first assignment, which I inherited when I started teaching English, is deeply problematic. It asks students to characterize a disabled adult character as being like a friend, child, or pet to the other main character in the book. Using SCAMPER helped me generate many possible

FIGURE 5.3

Example Assignment Brainstorms Using SCAMPER

Original Assignment	Write an essay about whether the relationship between George and Lennie in *Of Mice and Men* is most like that of two friends, a parent and child, or a caregiver and pet.	Interview someone about their experiences during the Cold War era. Write an article about how that person's experiences might inform our thinking and actions today.	Create an itinerary and budget to travel to a destination of your choice.
Substitute a different topic.	Write an essay comparing the relationship between George and Lennie to one of your own relationships.	Interview someone about their experiences on 9/11. Write an article about how that person's experiences might inform our thinking and actions today.	Create a carbon budget for traveling to and around a destination of your choice.
Combine the assignment with another assignment.	Write a series of vignettes showing how you relate to people in your life in different ways. (*Students also read* The House on Mango Street *and then wrote their own vignette collections.*)	Write an article based on your interview with someone about their experiences during the Cold War era; add their memories to the class timeline. (*Another unit task involved making a Cold War timeline.*)	After creating an itinerary and budget to travel to a destination of your choice, write a persuasive essay about why someone should travel there. (*Students wrote persuasive essays in their English classes.*)
Adjust the work product.	Write a comic portraying different ways George and Lennie relate to each other.	Interview someone about their experiences during the Cold War era. Make a collage using images from the interviewee's memories. Write an artist statement explaining how you represented your interviewee's experiences and how those experiences might inform your thinking and actions.	Create an itinerary and budget to show a visitor around our city.

Magnify or minify **the assignment, creating a larger or smaller version.**	Write an essay about something you think is true in relationships. Test the truth of your claim using the relationship between George and Lennie, the relationship between characters in another book, and a relationship between two people you know as evidence.	Choose a single event during the Cold War. Interview someone about their memories of that event, and write an article based on the interview.	Create an itinerary and budget for a one-day trip to a nearby destination of your choice.
Put the product to another use **within or beyond the classroom.**	Write a persuasive essay about how nondisabled adults should treat friends who have disabilities. Use the ways George treats Lennie as examples or as counterexamples to support your claims.	Interview someone about their experiences during the Cold War era. Working with a small group, make a podcast using clips from all your interviews, describing patterns and outliers among your interviewees' experiences. Conclude the podcast with ideas for how the various interviewees' experiences might inform our thinking and actions today.	Create an itinerary and budget to travel to a destination of your choice. Compare yours with a partner's and evaluate advantages and disadvantages of each one.
Eliminate one of the assignment's requirements.	Write an essay analyzing any relationship in *Of Mice and Men*.	Interview someone about their experiences during the Cold War.	Create an itinerary and budget for one aspect of traveling—such as adventure, food, or art—in a destination of your choice.
Reverse **the assignment in some way.**	Assess these three essays, each of which makes a different point about the relationship between George and Lennie. In your comments, explain whether and why you found the essayist's argument convincing.	Make a list of questions you have about the Cold War era. Ask someone who remembers the Cold War era what lingering questions they have about it. Write an essay comparing and contrasting their questions to yours.	Make a dream itinerary of activities you'd enjoy, match it to a destination, and figure out the cost.

alternatives, any of which would have been an improvement. However, even if an assignment is acceptable and produces good assessment evidence—as was the case for the other two assignments—you might imagine alternative or additional assignments that would be even more effective and affirming.

Generative tools such as SCAMPER are designed to help you come up with many different ideas. Some of those ideas will almost certainly work better than others in your classroom. Figure 5.4 offers an evaluation tool you can use to decide whether to give a particular assignment. It asks questions about the assignment itself, its instructional and assessment functions, and its potential to be meaningful work for students.

Throughout this chapter, I've offered different examples of assignments (paint a fantasy version of the view from one's bedroom window, create a carbon budget for traveling to and around the destination of your choice, create a Spanish how-to video showing how to prepare a favorite healthy snack, and so on). I hope these examples have helped you get a sense of what an affirming assignment sounds like. However, all the questions on the evaluation tool (Figure 5.4) ask about what your assignment *does*, as opposed to what it *is*. An affirming assignment is defined not by its form but by its functions—how it creates opportunities for students to do work they find important and fulfilling.

Onward

This chapter was about how to design assignments that affirm students' identities, strengths, and values by asking them to do work that matters—to them personally and in the world. However, an affirming assignment is only an opportunity for students to do meaningful work. They don't always take advantage of that opportunity. Sometimes they do whatever seems easy or comfortable in the moment. The next chapter is about how to design work processes that help students bring themselves more fully to their work.

FIGURE 5.4
Assignment Evaluation Tool

Assignment Statement

Describe the assignment in one or two sentences. A clear assignment statement helps your students understand exactly what they're being asked to do.

Assessment Functions

How will this product or performance demonstrate what students know and can do?

What important skills and knowledge *won't* students be able to demonstrate through this product or performance?

Instructional Functions

What academic skills and knowledge will students develop in the process of creating this product or performance?

What relational skills and knowledge will students develop in the process of creating this product or performance?

Real-World Contributions

What audience will potentially encounter this product or performance?

How might this product or performance benefit the community?

Self-Expression

How will this assignment provide opportunities for students to share their own stories or develop their own ideas?

How will this assignment provide opportunities for students to discover their own voices—that is, figure out a style of communication that feels authentic for them?

Self-Making

What decisions will students make while working on this assignment?

How might making these decisions help students discover values they want to live by?

6

Empowering Work Processes

The assignment was "Write an essay exploring your relationship with someone or something in your neighborhood that matters to you." Unlike five-paragraph analytical essays, personal essays that explore the author's relationship with a place exist in the literary world. The topic was specific enough that students understood exactly what they were being asked to do but still broad enough to connect to in personal ways. If they wanted to, students could submit their essays to local newspapers so more people could read them. The neighborhood essay checked all the boxes of an affirming assignment. I thought my students would produce good writing and feel the satisfaction that comes from doing meaningful work. I was wrong.

Two students wrote about the same local playground, and the difference between their essays was revealing. One student, whom I'll call Josiah, wrote about how his cousin dared him to jump off the swings. The playground, he wrote, was where he learned the difference between daring and courage, because courage sometimes meant standing up for himself and *not* doing the daring thing. Another student, whom I'll call Sari, wrote about how the playground is a fun place to play. The slide is fun. The swings are fun. Running is fun.

There were more essays like Josiah's. Romy wrote about how an oddly painted fire hydrant made her wonder how she could make boring parts of life more interesting. Winston wrote about new construction in Harlem—how it represented gentrification and made him want to embrace both his own Blackness and the white German side of his family, even as he rejected white appropriation. At 12 years old, Winston was still developing the skills he needed to explain his sophisticated ideas, but he was saying something important about the world and his place in it.

If students like Romy, Winston, and Josiah could write about deep and personal relationships with their neighborhoods, even as they struggled with other aspects of writing, why had most of my students written about having fun at the local playground, liking the falafel at a local restaurant, or seeing trash in the Hudson River but couldn't articulate a relationship with the place, much less explain how that relationship affected them?

Perhaps you've had a similar experience. Perhaps you designed an assignment you thought would inspire amazing work and felt disappointed when it didn't. Perhaps you've seen students pick topics that seemed easy or funny but held little if any personal meaning. Perhaps you've seen students pick a format or style that seemed obvious or comfortable, rather than choosing their own way to approach their work. Perhaps you've seen students turn in a first draft because they didn't think revising was worth the effort.

As frustrating as this is for teachers, it's also a missed opportunity for students. Even when they get a great assignment, students don't always make it meaningful. This chapter is about why—and how we can empower students to bring more of themselves to their work.

Why Students Don't Make Their Work Meaningful

The phrase *crisis of conscience* sounds a little dramatic, but that's how I felt when I read the neighborhood essays. I worked so hard to write assignments that invited students to explore what was important to them. Why had so many of them declined the invitation?

When I talked about this problem with my colleagues, more than one told me to lower my expectations. They said some students just didn't think that deeply or work that hard but I rejected this deficit thinking. Every student is capable of feeling the full range of human emotions, being curious about themselves and the world, having important ideas, and expressing those ideas creatively. The fact that they *weren't* was not evidence that they *couldn't* under different circumstances. But what were those circumstances?

Other colleagues suggested that if I wanted students to write about what was most important to them, I should only give *A*s to students who did. I was just as horrified by the notion of using grades to compel students to bare their souls as I was by the notion that some students didn't have souls to bare. If my students were going to write about what mattered to them, it would be because they genuinely wanted to.

I wondered if the problem was me. Did my students feel unsafe writing about what mattered most to them? Many students who'd written flat essays about trivial topics had opened up to me in other ways. They'd hung back after class or shown up during their lunch periods to talk about their lives. They'd sought my help with personal conflicts. I have no doubt I needed to work on my relationships with students because most of us do, but that didn't feel like a sufficient explanation for why so many of them weren't going deep in their writing.

I wondered if the problem was school. I taught 7th grade, which meant my students had at least seven years' worth of messages to sit down, be quiet, and comply with expectations. Even if they felt safe with me, many (if not most) of my students had learned to please others—not to make their work meaningful and satisfying for themselves. I couldn't undo that learning history, so what *could* I do to encourage students to bring more of themselves to their work without making them feel like they had to?

Teaching Students to Bring Themselves to Their Work

At a professional learning workshop during the summer of 2013, I had a conversation I count as one of the truly transformative moments of my teaching career. My colleague, Kate, listened patiently as I described the neighborhood essay assignment, how my students had missed the opportunity to make it meaningful, and all the ways I'd tried and failed to explain the problem. Then Kate asked the question that changed me as an educator: "Did you *teach them how* to bring themselves to their writing?"

Wow. No. I did not.

Have you ever been in someone else's house and struggled to open the door? There are two locks and you only opened one, or the door sticks and you have to push hard, or push up while you turn the knob, or pull the knob while you push the door, or use a key you have to jiggle. You had no way of knowing any of this, but you feel helpless and stuck until the other person opens the door for you, and then you just feel embarrassed. Maybe you make a joke like "I promise, I know how to open doors," but you sort of feel like you don't.

I had, in effect, given my students many doors to meaningful work, but I hadn't taught them how to open those doors. Some had managed to get them open, but others—most of the class—just opened the doors they already knew how to open, even if they led to a less satisfying experience.

Just as we need to teach students how to use commas and factor polynomials, we need to teach them how to make their schoolwork meaningful. The rest of this chapter describes processes you can use to empower students to bring more of themselves to their work. We'll see how to help students select a personally significant topic, develop a voice within the discipline, and revise their work in accordance with their values—all while adhering to the assignment guidelines.

Topic Selection

During my 18 years as a teacher, I saw a lot of student work about pizza. Multiple students wrote their neighborhood essays about how their local pizzeria serves the best pizza. I've seen students research pizza history, calculate pizza geometry, and create two- and three-dimensional pizza art. However, just because students like to eat pizza does not mean they have something important to communicate about pizza—or that a school project on pizza will be a source of vitality and satisfaction.

If students pick their own topics for an assignment, some will select topics that deeply matter to them. Others will select whatever topic seems obvious, easy, familiar, or amusing. The following process helps students figure out which topic truly matters to them.

Student Task #1: Generate a Long List of Potential Topics

If we want students to make a meaningful selection, they need many options from which to select. Sometimes we provide a list of potential topics, but if we're looking to tap into students' existing interests and knowledge, we need ways to get them to generate lists themselves. Try one of these strategies:

- **Set a target number of items for students to list.** For the neighborhood essay, I started asking students to write the name of their neighborhood and then add the words *17 things I know about* to the beginning. They ended up with phrases such as "17 things I know about Tribeca" or "17 things I know about New Rochelle." Having a large target number pushes students past the first few things they notice and helps them think of less immediately obvious but potentially more interesting things they know.

- **Give a sentence starter, set a timer, and tell students they have that long to list as many ways as possible to complete the sentence.** When I assigned an essay about students' intersecting identities, I wrote "I am . . ." on the board, set a timer for two minutes, and had students list as many ways to complete the sentence as they could think of within that time. Although they made their lists in the privacy of their notebooks, I made my own list on the board, both to indicate the kinds of things they could write and to show them I wasn't asking them to do something I wasn't willing to do, too. Your sentence starter will depend on your assignment topic, and the amount of time you set will depend on your students' needs.

- **Give specific prompts, two or three at a time, to help students remember diverse experiences.** When I assigned an essay about memorable experiences with food, I wanted my students to be able to choose a food memory that mattered to them, which meant they had to remember many different food experiences. Food is such a broad topic, though, and if I'd simply asked them to list food memories, some students might only list certain kinds of food memories or feel so overwhelmed that they struggled to remember anything. I needed to ask diverse, specific questions to elicit diverse, specific memories. Figure 6.1 includes all the prompts I gave my students to help them remember personal stories about food. Notice that the prompts are grouped into sets of two or three. Giving prompts two or three at a time gets them to linger over prompts they might give up on if they had a longer list, but if a certain prompt completely stumps them, they have one or two more they can use.

FIGURE 6.1

Examples of Specific Prompts to Help Students Generate Potential Topics

What are your stories about . . .

- Cooking with family or friends?
- Cooking by yourself?
- Cooking mistakes (your own or someone else's)?

- Holiday meals?
- Restaurant meals?
- School meals?

- Shopping for food?
- Growing or gathering food?

- Eating in a familiar place?
- Eating in a new place (such as while traveling, being outdoors, in a new home, or at a new friend's house)?

- Trying a new food?
- Changing your mind about a particular type of food?

- Getting sick of a particular food?
- Getting sick from a particular food?

- Religious or ethical food choices?
- Arguments or conflicts about food?
- Food comforting you during a difficult time?

- **Involve family members who might recall topics or experiences the student might not think of.** When I taught 2nd grade, my students wrote in journals almost every day. At first, I either gave a story starter or told them to write about whatever they wanted. Most students wrote *something* but not necessarily something they found meaningful. I decided to enlist support from the people who knew my students best: their families. I sent home a letter asking parents and guardians to write topics their kids would find meaningful on little slips of paper. It didn't matter if anyone else would understand the topic's significance—only that the child would. I put the slips into a little paper bag with that student's name, and whenever they wanted a topic to write about, the student could pull one from their writing grab-bag. Involving families doesn't have to be an elaborate process. Sending an email about an upcoming assignment and encouraging families to think about what would be interesting to their kids is often enough.

Student Task #2: Articulate a Personal Connection to Each Item

If we want our students to work with topics that matter to them personally, we need to ensure they discover those personal connections. After students have made their lists of potential topics, ask them to follow each item with a sentence that begins with the word *I* or *My* and describes some way they are connected to that item.

Imagine, for example, that a student is making a list of 17 things she knows about her neighborhood. One item on her list is "El Barrio has awesome churro fries." She's made a small personal connection already because *awesome* is her opinion, but if prompted to add a statement of personal connection beginning with *I* or *My*, she might write, "My dad usually stuffs half of them into his face before my mom and I can eat one." She's now found a personal connection to El Barrio that goes a bit deeper than liking their churro fries.

Student Task #3: Sort the Connections According to How Personally Meaningful They Are

Imagine that an earth science class will choose environmental pollutants to research and then write letters to local legislators. In preparation, one student lists pollutants he's heard about and then adds personal connections. His list might include things like "Mercury: *I* eat fish that probably contains it," "Carbon dioxide: *I* am affected by global warming," "Glyphosate: *My* good friend had cancer in 6th grade, and glyphosate is a carcinogen," and "Antidepressants: *I* take Lexapro, and I just read something about how antidepressants are in rivers."

All these pollutants matter, but the student's connections to certain ones seem stronger and more personal. Sorting the connections—as opposed to the topics themselves—helps the student choose a topic that resonates with him.

Depending on your assignment, you might have students sort their personal connections as fleeting versus lasting, shallow versus deep, strong versus weak, major versus minor, or life-altering versus inconsequential. They could sort the connections into two groups, add a category in between, or rate them on a scale between two extremes. If they write their items on sticky notes, students can rearrange them into piles or along a continuum.

Student Task #4: Test the Topics to Determine Which One Works Best for the Student and the Assignment

Perhaps you've seen students pick topics they seemed super-excited about, but when they started working, that energy fizzled. If students begin their project in a few different ways—for example, by outlining two different essays or sketching three different fantasy versions of the same landscape—they can experience how important each one feels before deciding which topic is worth their sustained effort.

Depending on the project, you might have students begin several different pieces of work and then pick one to finish, or they could quickly make several simple prototypes and then pick one to make a larger and more complicated version of. Imagine that in a history class, students are researching abolitionists, designing awards named after them, and writing speeches nominating someone for the award. Students could imagine awards named after three different abolitionists before committing to one for their project. In a health class, students could record themselves making several different nutritious snacks before deciding on one video to reshoot, edit, and post to social media.

Student Task #5: Choose Which Project They Feel Most Compelled to Work On

Now that they've discovered potential topics, found personal connections to each one, evaluated those connections, and tested how it feels to work with topics they are the most connected to, students are finally ready to make a final selection!

This topic selection process might sound elaborate, but it doesn't have to be time-consuming. For the neighborhood essay, my students spent five minutes listing things they knew about their neighborhoods, another five minutes adding their personal connections in sentences beginning with *I* or *My*, and yet another five minutes rating their connections based on how deep and lasting they were. Students then chose three highly rated items and described those people, places, or things to a partner. By the end of the period, students knew which topic felt important enough to write an essay about.

You don't have to do all five steps of the topic selection process for every assignment. (I didn't!) You know your students best, and you have limited time with them, so you're in the best position to decide which steps to use and how to implement them. However, the more of this process students do, the more likely they are to select topics they find genuinely meaningful and therefore derive satisfaction from their work.

Exemplar Analysis

As a student, I wrote countless essays before ever reading a published one. Instead of analyzing excellent essays and discovering structures and styles I could use, I was given rules and formulas: the first paragraph should introduce the topic and end with a thesis statement, the next three paragraphs should make supporting points and cite evidence, and the last paragraph should summarize the argument. No wonder the essays I wrote for school all sound stilted and empty.

Other assignments asked me to make types of work I'd seen before, but I didn't know what made the good ones good. During my time as a student, my peers and I had to make posters about countries, animals, elements, biographies, geometry proofs, and Latin noun declensions. Each time, we cut letters from construction paper and pictures from magazines (it was the 80s), printed out paragraphs we'd probably plagiarized, and glued it all to a piece of posterboard—but not once did we spend time looking at actual posters or discussing what constitutes a good one.

When students have an assignment, they benefit from seeing and analyzing *exemplars*: excellent work of the type they're about to create. To make an effective poster about a geometry proof, students need to know about the proof *and* understand what makes a poster eye-catching, clear, and instructive. Therefore, in addition to learning about proofs (which presumably happens through their geometry lessons and independent research), they'd need to read and analyze informational posters. The geometry teacher might not see poster-making skills as relevant to learning math, but students are better equipped to do excellent work when they've seen what excellence looks like.

Using Exemplars

Ensuring students can do excellent work seems like enough of a reason to give them exemplars, but looking at them has additional benefits. Work products reflect what's important to the people who created them. By analyzing a piece of excellent work (whether it's a poster, an essay, or anything else), students can discover how it reflects what matters to the person who created it—and how they can make their schoolwork reflect what matters to them.

Moreover, when students look at multiple, diverse exemplars, they can abstract what all work of that type *must* include while discovering possibilities for what it *can* include. For example, if students look at several different informational posters, they might notice various color schemes, fonts, shapes, graphic styles, and amounts of explanatory text. They might also notice that every poster uses contrasting colors to draw the viewer's eye, fonts that distinguish titles from body text (yet are both easy to read), a balance of visual and verbal elements, and empty space. When all exemplars have a certain feature, students' work will need to have that feature, too. Conversely, when there is a range of possibilities, students have a choice—and can choose to approach their work in a way that's consistent with their values.

Finding Exemplars

If you ask students to create the sort of work that exists in the real world, you should be able to find multiple exemplars. However, what qualifies as an exemplar, how many you use, and how diverse they are will depend on the assignment and your students' needs.

For example, NPR (2022) had a long-running special series called "Three Books," in which they posted reviews of three different books united by a single theme. When my colleague and I stumbled on these, we decided to have our students write their own three-book reviews. For this assignment, all the exemplars came from NPR because it was a genre unique to them. However, rather than having our students scroll through dozens of reviews, we selected a few that showed a range of themes and writing styles. If our assignment had been to review only one book, we would have pulled book reviews from multiple sites.

Asking Questions About Exemplars

When I simply gave my students a set of exemplars—three-book reviews, essays, or whatever they would be making—they often spontaneously judged which ones they liked and didn't like. They needed explicit guidance to look closely at each exemplar and discover how it reflects what matters to its creator, which helped them imagine how to make their own work reflect what matters to them. Breaking the process of exemplar analysis into two stages helped students consider each exemplar on its own terms (stage 1) before comparing, contrasting, and judging them (stage 2).

Figures 6.2 and 6.3 offer questions for the two stages of exemplar analysis. Whether you put the questions on the board or use handouts, have students complete stage 1 before giving them the questions for stage 2.

Your students could answer the exemplar analysis questions in writing, on a graphic organizer (such as a chart for stage 1 and a Venn diagram for stage 2), in conversations with partners, or in a whole-class discussion.

FIGURE 6.2

Exemplar Analysis Questions for Stage 1

Looking at each exemplar,

- **Observe:** What did the person who created this do? Note details or features that stand out.
- **Acknowledge:** What's interesting about those choices?
- **Critique:** What, if anything, is ineffective or off-putting about those choices?
- **Interpret:** What seems important to the person who created this? What do they want the people who encounter it to think about or do?

Source: Adapted from *Two-for-One Teaching*, by L. Porosoff and J. Weinstein, 2020, Solution Tree. Copyright 2020 by Solution Tree.

My students responded to the stage 1 questions in their notebooks, then had a whole-class discussion responding to the *compare* and *contrast* questions in stage 2. Finally, they talked to partners about their responses to the *choose* question—and then they got to work.

The exemplar analysis questions apply to almost any type of work, but you might use language that applies to your specific assignment. Instead of "the person who created this," you might say "the researcher," "the composer," or "the game designer." Instead of "this type of product or performance," you might say "three-book reviews," "posters," "how-to videos," or whatever your students are about to make. Even though my students needed an entire class period to analyze exemplars, we did it during every project because it helped them see their work as an expression of their values.

FIGURE 6.3

Exemplar Analysis Questions for Stage 2

Based on what you saw across all the exemplars,

- **Compare:** What features do these have in common? What seems to be a requirement of this type of product or performance?
- **Contrast:** What interesting differences exist? What seems to be possible in this type of product or performance?
- **Choose:** What do you want to do in your work so it reflects what's important to you?

Source: Adapted from *Two-for-One Teaching*, by L. Porosoff and J. Weinstein, 2020, Solution Tree. Copyright 2020 by Solution Tree.

Responsive Feedback

One time in a faculty meeting, an administrator explained that when giving feedback to students, we should "describe and prescribe": say what the student did well and poorly, then say what they should do to improve.

Describe and prescribe. It sounded catchy. It also reflected recommendations from education professors John Hattie and Helen Timperley (2007), who assert that feedback exists to "reduce the gap between current and desired understandings" (p. 86), so teachers should "assist in identifying these gaps [and] provide remediation in the form of alternative or other steps" (p. 102).

Other scholars have expanded on Hattie and Timperley's work. Education professor Lia Voerman and her colleagues (2014) argue that in addition to describing gaps between actual and expected knowledge, teachers should describe the student's progress from past to present knowledge because that's more motivating. Educator Zaretta Hammond (2015) developed a feedback protocol that includes building trust-based relationships, communicating high expectations and the student's ability to achieve them, describing the student's work as compared to the goal, prescribing next steps for improvement, and giving more encouragement. These frameworks make the feedback process more equitable and supportive, yet they still involve describing and prescribing.

Well, not really. If we're telling students what they did well and poorly, whether compared to past performance or extrinsic expectations, we're not so much describing the work as evaluating it. *Evaluate and prescribe* doesn't quite roll off the tongue, but that's what we're doing. Evaluative feedback communicates what the person giving it thinks is good, and prescriptive feedback communicates what the person giving it thinks should happen.

Evaluative and prescriptive feedback helps students learn (Wisniewski, Zierer, & Hattie, 2020). However, when people do work they find important, they're looking for a response. They want the people who encounter their work to notice important details, ask important questions, and do something important as a result of the encounter—even if the "something important" is simply to think, remember, imagine, feel, talk, or listen. Especially then.

Figure 6.4 has questions to guide responsive feedback. It's designed as a graphic organizer to help students use it when peer-reviewing one another's

FIGURE 6.4

Giving Responsive Feedback

Feedback Giver	Feedback Receiver
Observations	**Questions**
Which details stand out to you? List the details. If a detail evokes a specific emotion, image, or memory, please tell me what it is. Please do not indicate which parts you like or dislike—only what you feel, imagine, or remember as you encounter them.	What questions do you have about my work as a whole or any part of it? List your questions. • Questions that begin with WHAT or WHICH will help me add details. • Questions that begin with WHEN or WHERE will help me add context. • Questions that begin with HOW or WHY will help me add explanation.
Interpretations	**Inspirations**
What seems important to me? Don't worry if you're wrong, and don't ask me to interpret my work for you. The more you tell me about what seems important to me, the better I'll understand what's getting across.	What does my work make you want to do? For example, is there something I did in my work that you want to do in yours? Did I raise a topic or an issue you want to explore further? Did I show you a place you want to visit or an action you want to take?

Source: Adapted from *Two-for-One Teaching*, by L. Porosoff and J. Weinstein, 2020, Solution Tree. Copyright 2020 by Solution Tree.

work, but you can use it, too. You can even send it to parents and guardians, who often want to see their kids' work but don't always know what kinds of feedback to give (and usually end up giving evaluative and prescriptive feedback, because that's what they received as students).

The feedback form includes space to write, but reviewers could write on a separate sheet or in an electronic document, or you could create an online form with the questions. Written feedback provides each student with a record, in the reviewer's words, of how that person experienced their work.

If you can spare the class time, have at least two different reviewers give responsive feedback to each student. Different people will have different responses, showing students various ways their audience experiences their product or performance—and empowering them to make values-based decisions about their work.

After receiving feedback from one or more peers (and perhaps from one or more adults), ask your students to notice how they feel, physically and emotionally, as they read it. In particular, they should notice any discomfort: disappointment, sadness, embarrassment, anger, disgust, or perhaps some muscle tension, queasiness, or a faster heartbeat. Unpleasant as these emotions and sensations are, they tell students that their work didn't create the response they wanted. Something important *isn't* happening. If the idea they wanted to communicate isn't quite what they got across, students now have an opportunity to revise. Figure 6.5 offers prompts to help them use responsive feedback to revise their work so it has the impact they want it to have.

Responsive feedback gives students information about a discrepancy, not between their performance and a predefined learning goal but between their work's intended and actual impact. Unlike evaluative and prescriptive feedback, which position the giver as an authority who decides how good the work is and what the student should do, responsive feedback positions the giver as a fellow human who has a psychological experience of the student's work. Finally, whereas evaluative and prescriptive feedback help students understand what to change so their work better meets extrinsic standards, responsive feedback helps them discover what they want to change so their work has an effect they think is important.

FIGURE 6.5

Using Responsive Feedback

Using the Observations	Using the Questions
• Are the details that stood out the ones you think *should* stand out? If not, consider cutting those details or adding more detail to the parts you want to stand out more. • Did the details evoke the kinds of emotions, images, or memories you want to evoke? If not, consider changing the language or tone you use to express them.	• Based on the questions, — What details might you add? Would they satisfy the audience's curiosity or just distract them from the main point? — What context might you include? Would that be helpful information or just a distraction? — What could you explain more fully? • Do any questions indicate parts that are confusing or misleading? Consider clarifying those parts.
Using the Interpretations	**Using the Inspirations**
Look at the things your reviewers said *seemed* important to you. Are those things *actually* important to you? If not, consider expanding or clarifying parts that indicate what *is* important to you. Also consider removing anything that will lead the audience to believe you think something is important but you actually don't.	Look at the things your work made reviewers want to do. Are those the sorts of actions that matter to you? People do things based on *their* wants, needs, and values. Keeping that in mind, consider removing or changing certain parts, and adding others, so your work inspires people to do the sorts of things *you* think are important.

Source: Adapted from *Two-for-One Teaching*, by L. Porosoff and J. Weinstein, 2020, Solution Tree. Copyright 2020 by Solution Tree.

Staging the Work Process

We've now seen how to help students find topics that matter to them, create excellent work that reflects their values, and revise their work so it has a meaningful impact. These are all ways students can bring more of themselves to their schoolwork.

Still, it's schoolwork. The teacher assigns and assesses it based on what students are expected to know and be able to do. If we don't communicate our expectations, we're denying our students the opportunity to succeed. However, if we tell our students what we expect, we make our goal their goal. According to psychology researchers, when someone has a goal, they tend to focus narrowly on achieving it (Gilbert, 2010; Villatte et al., 2016; Wilson & DuFrene, 2009). As soon as our students know what we want, they'll look for the quickest and easiest way to please us, get a good grade, and feel the relief of having finished—even at the expense of doing work they find important and satisfying.

We now have a dilemma. If we don't tell our students what we expect, we create inequity, but if we do tell our students what we expect, we get compliance. How can we ensure our students have equitable access to everything they need to achieve success while also ensuring they can experience the vitality that comes from doing meaningful work?

Three important ways teachers share expectations with students are through assignments, success criteria, and evaluative feedback. We can delay giving each of these to students until after they've discovered how they can bring their values to the work.

First, we can delay giving the assignment until *after* students have gone through the topic selection process so students choose topics based on what's important to them rather than on what they think of most quickly when they receive the assignment. For example, students can figure out an important connection to a person, place, or thing in their neighborhoods before they know they'll be writing an essay about it. By the time they get the assignment, they've already started working on it in a way that matters to them.

Next, we can delay sharing success criteria until *after* students have analyzed diverse exemplars and discovered for themselves what's required and what's possible. By the time they get our criteria, students have seen many ways to meet those criteria and have begun visualizing their own approach.

Finally, we can delay giving evaluative feedback until *after* students have received responsive feedback and used it to guide their revisions so their work makes an impact they think is important. Then we can tell them how well their work matches our criteria and suggest changes. In other words, students first bring their product or performance into alignment with their own values and then ensure it also aligns with predefined standards of excellence.

If we guide students toward meeting our expectations without initially telling them what those expectations are, they can achieve excellence and pursue what's important to them. We're assessing their product or performance, but the experience of working on it becomes less about showing what they know and more about serving their values.

The timeline in Figure 6.6 shows how to stage the work process to maximize opportunities for students to make their work meaningful. The left side shows when to provide various resources, strategies, and feedback. These givens promote equity by ensuring all students have access to everything they need to achieve excellence. On the right side, you'll see topic

FIGURE 6.6
Work Process Timeline

Givens for EQUITY	WORK PROCESS	Choices for VITALITY	
Assignment Statement ▶ Clearly articulates what sudents will do		What topic is most important for me to work with?	TOPIC SELECTION
Multiple Exemplars ▶ Shows diverse ways excellent work can look	PREPARE	How will this piece of work reflect who I am and what matters to me?	EXEMPLAR ANALYSIS
Success Criteria ▶ Describes excellence for this type of work		How will it reflect my capabilities?	
Necessary Materials ▶ Ensures all students can create excellent work	CREATE	How will I approach my work so it reflects what matters to me?	
Strategy Instruction ▶ Broadens repertoire needed to do excellent work		How will I approach challenges?	
Evaluative Feedback ▶ Tells students how close they are to excellence	REFINE	What impact do I want my work to make?	RESPONSIVE FEEDBACK
Prescriptive Feedback ▶ Tells students what to do to achieve excellence		What changes will I make so it has that impact?	
Available Audience ▶ Helps excellent work have a real-world impact	SHARE	How widely will I share my work?	

selection coming just before students receive the assignment, exemplar analysis coming just before they receive a list of success criteria from you, and responsive feedback coming just before they receive evaluative and prescriptive feedback. These three processes, along with any other opportunities for students to make values-based choices, empower students to find meaning and vitality in their work.

Onward

In this chapter, we saw how to design and stage the process of completing an assignment so students can bring more of themselves to their work. We also saw how you can make the work process equitable by giving students everything they need to achieve success. In the next chapter, we'll explore how you and your students can work together to define what *success* means.

7

Co-Constructed Definitions of Success

When I was in 5th grade, every time we did something right, my teacher—I'll call her Mrs. Rivkin—gave us points. Turned in the homework? Ten points. Got a perfect score on a spelling test? Twenty points. Lined up quietly? Five points. We'd write our points on notecards taped to the corners of our desks, and at the end of each week, whoever got the most points became Top Banana. Top Banana got to be line leader, choose the read-aloud, and select a little prize—an eraser or a finger puppet or a yo-yo—from Mrs. Rivkin's desk drawer.

It was February, and I'd never been Top Banana. Every week, I carefully added up my points, but someone else always had more.

One day, Mrs. Rivkin gave us a homework assignment to bring in a million of something. I loved to read, especially about science, and I knew I had more than a million cells. I decided to bring . . . me! I couldn't wait to hear what Mrs. Rivkin would say, and I squirmed in anticipation as we all shared our millions. One kid brought a container of sugar that she estimated had a million grains. Another kid had tried to print out a million letters but ran out of paper.

"Lauren?" Mrs. Rivkin finally said. "Did you bring something in?"

My big moment had come. "I brought myself. I have a million—actually, billions of cells!"

Mrs. Rivkin made a face and called on the next student. I didn't understand. Why wasn't she happy?

It turned out that Mrs. Rivkin had asked us to bring in a million of something to introduce a new unit—on cells. She explained, without looking at me even once, that our bodies are made up of billions of cells, and we'd be learning about cell structures and their functions.

Then she gave us our points. Ten million points to the kid who tried to print a million letters. Five million to the kid who estimated sugar grains. Everyone else got one million points—except me and a kid who never did homework. We got zero points because, according to Mrs. Rivkin, we didn't complete the assignment.

It's been more than 30 years since Mrs. Rivkin gave me zero points, but I still remember the way my hand hovered over the notecard taped to the corner of my desk, paralyzed with a kind of heartbreak I couldn't name. My curiosity about science, my enthusiasm for reading, and what I thought was an imaginative approach to the assignment counted for absolutely *nothing*. I felt like nothing.

Typically, students are considered successful in school when they attend class, contribute to discussions, complete their assignments, put forth effort, make friends, pursue athletic or artistic or civic interests, and help others. Sometimes they struggle to learn the material or have a conflict with a peer, but they seek support. They try new strategies and work through their problems. Students who are considered successful comply with our demands, and their work meets our expectations.

When Mrs. Rivkin asked her students to bring in a million of something, she probably didn't expect the *something* to be the student's own body—but that's exactly why I was so excited. I successfully brought in a million of something, but only Mrs. Rivkin's definition of success mattered. My definition mattered so little that I got zero points.

By 5th grade, I'd started to develop some of the values I have now: imagination, curiosity, and an enthusiasm for learning. However, the older I got, the less important imagination was at school. It only mattered on so-called creative writing assignments, and those became fewer and further between. Even curiosity and enthusiasm for learning only mattered when they led to an outcome, such as finding a key detail in a book, which led to a better essay, which led to a better grade.

What if we reimagined the definition of a successful student to mean one who brings their own values to their learning, work, and relationships at school? What if, in addition to meeting our expectations and receiving our assessment of their skills, students decide for themselves what's important for them to accomplish and how well they accomplished it?

This chapter is about how to clarify and communicate your definition of success, help students clarify and communicate their own definitions of success based on what matters to them, and create space for those definitions to coexist.

Noticing Successes in the Room

As teachers, we usually look for certain things when we observe students and their work. When I taught middle school English, I gave a variety of writing assignments—from essays to poems to dramatic scenes—but used the same four success criteria: sticking to a topic or thesis, including specific imagery, using a clear organizational structure, and proofreading. When students develop these four writing skills, they are better able to communicate their ideas to a reader. I don't think I was wrong to look for evidence of these skills in students' work.

The problem is that when we look for something, we become so selectively attentive to it that we miss other things that also matter. Psychologists Daniel Simons and Christopher Chabris (1999) demonstrated this phenomenon in a clever experiment you can try yourself if you search for their names on YouTube (Simons, 2010). For the experiment, you watch two teams warming up for a basketball game. One team wears black, and the other wears white. Your job is to count how many times players on the white team pass the ball. (Last chance to look up the video before I spoil the surprise ending!)

You concentrate on members of the white team, count their passes, and feel smart when you get the right answer. But then you're asked if you saw the gorilla! The video replays, and indeed, a person in a gorilla suit strolled across the court, and you didn't see it! You were so intently watching for players in white that your brain screened out anyone wearing black—including the person wearing the black gorilla costume.

In classrooms, selective attention to the things *we* value can keep us from noticing how our students bring *their* values to their actions and inter-actions. If I look for essays that stick to a single thesis, I might disregard intersecting lines of inquiry. If I look for concrete imagery, I might disregard abstract ideas. If I look for organized thinking, I might disregard associative thinking. If I look for adherence to the conventions of standard English, I might disregard the ways students draw language from their homes and invent their own ways of expressing ideas. I might not even see students' strengths, let alone appreciate them, if I'm looking for something else—and I might see the work as unsuccessful—or less successful than it could have been.

One way we can counteract our tendency to disregard that which we're not looking for is to name what we *are* looking for, consider what positive features our selective attention might prevent us from seeing, and inten-tionally look for those. Try this exercise:

1. List characteristics of what you consider to be good work—whether that's a work product students create or working behaviors they exhibit in your classroom.

2. Beside each item on your list, write something positive you might undervalue as a result of looking for that characteristic. For example, if it's important to you that students carefully solve math problems one step at a time on paper, then you might undervalue their ability to solve problems holistically in their heads. If it's important to you that class discussions are lively, then you might undervalue when students think quietly (with the liveliness happening in their heads).

3. Choose something you are at risk of undervaluing and intention-ally search for it the next time you observe your students or assess their work.

If you tried the exercise, what did you discover about your students? What did you discover about their work? What did you discover about yourself? Just because the thing we're looking for is good doesn't mean its opposite is bad. We can honor the ways our students bring their values to their work *and* our own expectations of excellence.

Using Rubrics

Even for a relatively simple assignment like "Bring in a million of something," students need to understand what success looks like in order to be successful. Can the million things be part of their bodies? Do the million things have to be tangible, or could it be a million sounds? Does each of the million things need to be visible on its own, or could it be a million molecules in a drop of water? Is more than a million things acceptable, or does it have to be exactly one million?

Any time we give an assignment, we need to clearly articulate what success means so students know what to strive for and so we can hold them accountable. We can also hold ourselves accountable; if we expect students to do something in order to be successful, then we need to teach them how to do it. If we *don't* define our expectations, we need to be prepared for students to decide for themselves what success means.

Rubrics articulate success criteria for assignments. Figure 7.1 shows a rubric from one of my 6th grade English assignments. During the unit, students read several essays that connected food stories to the authors' cultural identities. Then they wrote about their own food memories, connected the stories to their identities, and found recipes to accompany their essays.

The food memory essay rubric in Figure 7.1 is a single-point rubric (Fluckiger, 2010). That is, it describes one point in learning: proficiency. You might be more familiar with analytic rubrics (Nitko & Brookhart, 2007), which describe multiple levels of performance. Some analytic rubrics describe satisfactory and unsatisfactory performance, whereas others describe excellent, good, fair, and poor performance for each of several criteria. When you make a rubric, just describe what success entails so your students know what it will take to succeed.

FIGURE 7.1

Example Rubric

Food Memory Essay: Write an essay about how a personal experience with food connects to your identity. Accompany your story with a related recipe.

Elements	Basic	Effective	Exemplary
The essay sticks to a single **thesis**: how the food memory connects to your identity.			
Specific, detailed **images** help the reader visualize and relate to what happens in the story.			
The essay is **organized** in a way that helps the reader follow the ideas in it. Topics are presented in a logical order. Transitions help the reader move from one topic to the next and from the essay to the recipe.			
The essay and recipe are **easy to read**: they have clear sentences, considerate formatting, titles, and no errors in capitalization, punctuation, spelling, or grammar. The recipe is properly cited.			
The recipe clearly **relates** to the story.			

Source: Copyright 2023 by Lauren Porosoff.

Making Parallel Rubrics

The first writing assignment I gave my 6th graders was a poem about something they love to do. We would focus all year on using specific imagery to inform, involve, and convince the reader, and a poem seemed like a good way to begin practicing those skills. In class, we'd identified imagery in books and practiced strategies for creating verbal images. My rubric included only two success criteria: using specific imagery and proofreading. Simple enough.

Zohar was one of those kids who got excited about everything, including her poem. She had chosen to write about a family camping trip, which she told me all about. I kept trying to redirect her: "That sounds amazing. Make sure you put some of those details into your poem. I can't wait to read it."

When I did read her poem, I saw that Zohar hadn't fixed the capitalization and spelling mistakes she'd marked on a copy she'd insisted on printing out, and her document history revealed no substantive revisions at all.

It turned out that Zohar had spent most of her time finding a font that looked like tree branches and changing the colors on each line to mimic the spectacular sunset she'd witnessed but didn't mention in the poem. I sighed. The imagery was weak and the proofreading nonexistent. Zohar's work barely met the expectations I'd so clearly laid out in the rubric.

A few weeks after grading Zohar's poem, I was browsing Netflix and found the then-new show *Tidying Up with Marie Kondo*. It was the latest in a subgenre of reality shows about aesthetics, which exist for homes, fashion, food, makeup, and events. Aesthetics is kind of a big deal. It's a major branch of philosophy. Plato and Confucius wrote about aesthetics, and as far as we know, they didn't write about putting commas in the right places. I was Zohar's English teacher, and my job was to make sure she learned to proofread, but who decided that proofreading matters and font colors don't?

When we create a rubric, we communicate what we think is important. If we ask students to create their own rubrics, we are giving them an opportunity to communicate what they think is important. Try this: after students look at exemplars, but before they look at your rubric, ask what they want to accomplish. What will the work look like if it represents what's important to them? What qualities do they most want to bring to the process? Have students articulate their answers as success criteria that they put on their own rubrics, which can exist alongside yours.

Figure 7.2 shows what a student-made rubric might look like. In this example, Zohar's essay was about a time when two friends came over and

FIGURE 7.2
Example Student-Made Rubric

Food Memory Essay: Write an essay about how a personal experience with food connects to your identity. Accompany your story with a related recipe.

Elements	Basic	Effective	Exemplary
The story is funny.			
You can tell my friends are really close and I love them.			
My story sounds like I'm the one who wrote it. It doesn't sound like a robot wrote it.			
I used a font that relates to the story.			

they ended up playfighting with Cheerios. The essay was full of punctuation mistakes and had no paragraph breaks, and because it only told the story and didn't include a thesis, it wasn't really an essay at all. The recipe, instead of being for something that uses Cheerios, was for lasagna, because that's what Zohar ate for dinner after her friends went home. It wasn't a very successful essay by my standards—but by hers? It was warm and funny, like she was. It conveyed how much she loved and cared about her friends and the closeness among them. It had voice. And yes, its font had big round puffy letters that looked like Cheerios. Zohar was very proud of her work and showed it to her friends who started reminiscing about that day. Would you call that successful writing?

Some students will discover features of successful work in the process of working. My older child, Kalino, was once working on a drawing of atomic structure when suddenly the subatomic particles made them think of the two presidential candidates at the time. (The nucleus was the candidate who wanted to be the center of attention, and the electron shell was the candidate who wanted to share and collaborate.) Once Kalino had that idea, they wanted their drawing to be funny and make a political statement in addition to showing scientific information.

As students work and discover qualities that feel important, encourage them to modify their rubrics. It wouldn't be fair if you were to change your rubric while students are in the middle of the project, but you can tell them about modifications you've made over the years or how you modified a rubric you found. That shows how definitions of success are provisional, contextual, and flexible—and that just as you can generate and revise your definition of success, so can they.

Some students might have difficulty articulating a definition of success for themselves. These students are often the ones who are laser-focused on satisfying the teacher's expectations so they can get a good grade, or they're the ones who have a history of doing poorly in school and are just trying to survive it. Either way, they are so caught up in someone else's definition of success that they can't imagine their own, and even trying can be intimidating.

If students struggle to make their own rubric, you might be tempted to tell them what matters to them, based on your own observations of their work and behavior. These suggestions might help, but you might misinterpret what's important to them or describe what you think should be important to them. If you offer students language to help them describe their success criteria, be clear that you're not sure and might be wrong. You could say something like, "I've seen you making connections between the stuff we learn in class and the stuff you see in the news. Would it be fair to say that making those connections is part of what makes you feel successful in this class?"

Some students might resist any help you offer; they might not be ready to name or even notice the ways they could feel successful in class. They might have a history of experiencing school as so negative that they're not ready to consider how it could be positive. Don't push too hard. Instead, just keep offering them opportunities to create parallel rubrics. Even if they never write anything, they'll see their peers creating definitions of success and might start to believe it's possible for them to do it too.

Using Parallel Rubrics

Parallel rubrics help students assess their own actions as they work. At any point, they can ask themselves two fundamental questions:

- Is what I'm doing right now moving me closer to or further from my definition of success?
- Is what I'm doing right now moving me closer to or further from my teacher's definition of success?

If their actions will help them succeed by both definitions, great! If their actions won't help them succeed by either definition, why are they doing whatever they're doing? Many students won't need this question; just asking if their actions are moving them closer to either or both definitions of success often prompts them to get back on task.

If their actions will help them succeed by only their own definition or only yours, they can try to find a different way forward so they meet both sets of expectations—or they can proceed, knowing their actions will help them meet one set of expectations but not the other. One definition of success isn't better or more valid than another; the definitions exist concurrently.

FIGURE 7.3

Example Parallel Rubrics for Class Participation

Elements of Participation	Basic	Effective	Exemplary
I bring my readings and note-taking materials to every class.			
I listen actively during discussions.			
I ask relevant questions.			
I take detailed notes.			
During lab, I follow rules and procedures carefully.			
My lab partner and I split up the work fairly.			
My lab partner and I listen to each other.			
My drawings are on topic. They're not just random doodles.			
My notes are color-coded by topic.			
I relate what we're learning to pop culture references and the news.			

With an awareness of these multiple and coexisting definitions of success, students can choose at any given moment to act on one, the other, or both. Figure 7.3 shows parallel rubrics for participation in a high school science class.

A rubric that reflects the student's values does not negate or diminish your rubric. If anything, students might see your rubric as the "real" one, and you'll have to show them—through your comments and conversations—that their success criteria matter just as much as yours. The goal isn't to convince them of which criteria matter most; it's to teach students how to choose their actions based on multiple sets of criteria.

Feedback That Honors Students' Humanity

The feedback you give students can help them understand themselves—as learners and as people. If you use your own rubric, filling it out lets students know how well they demonstrated a skill you value (or that's valued in the community you represent). If you collect and fill out student-made rubrics, then you're showing students how well you think they demonstrated the skills they value.

Nevertheless, a rubric is most useful to students while they're working so they remain aware of expectations. After they've completed the work, a rubric becomes a tool we use to express judgments about how successfully students met expectations. When students read a rubric we've filled out, they might feel

- Happy if we say they were successful.
- Sad if we say they were unsuccessful.
- Frustrated if they tried but failed to meet our criteria for success.
- Surprised if they hadn't expected us to think they were successful.
- Angry if they think they were successful but we don't.
- Guilty if they think they didn't try hard enough to achieve success.
- Ashamed if they think they'll never be successful.

In any of these cases, our students' feelings depend on the extent to which they've pleased us. It's normal for people to want to please members of their community, but finding out how pleased we are doesn't have to be the only outcome of reading our feedback. Our feedback can also help students become more aware of their own values and how they can bring their values to future endeavors within and beyond your class. You can foster that awareness by sharing your observations, your personal experience of their work, your interpretations of their values, and your suggestions for their continued growth in areas that matter.

Making Observations

What did you see and hear? When we look at student work, it's usually through the lens of our own expectations. It's easy to skip past observing to judging: what we liked and didn't like, what we found effective and ineffective, and what we think the student should and shouldn't do in the future. We need to slow down if we want to truly see the work. What details stand out? What patterns can we detect? What larger issues or questions does this seem connected to?

Most teachers find assessing student work tedious (I certainly do), and many books describe how to make the process go faster. If we make observations, the assessment process takes more time—there are no tricks to get around that—but when you've pointed out meaningful aspects of students' work, they'll know you've truly seen them. Feeling seen is an essential aspect of belonging to a community, which is satisfying by itself. If you take time to see things that matter to students, imagine how satisfying that will feel for them. You might also find, as I did, that fully seeing students for who they are makes your work more satisfying, too.

Sharing Your Experience of the Work

What did you think about and feel? As you observe students' work and describe what you see, you can also share the thoughts, memories, or emotions it evokes. Zohar's Cheerios story reminded me of making popcorn with a childhood friend. Maybe Kalino's political cartoon about atomic structure made their science teacher laugh and contemplate a serious issue at the same time. Sharing how their work affects us shows students that their work can have an impact. The work also becomes a jumping-off point for us to share our feelings, stories, and ideas with our students.

Interpreting the Student's Values

What does it seem like this student cares about? When looking at a student's work, we can point out people, places, issues, events, actions, or qualities that seem important to that student. If a student keeps coming back to the same topic—camping, friends, politics, geography, trans rights—point it out, but make clear that you're inferring their values from direct observations and that your interpretation might be wrong: "*I noticed* that both your poem and your essay are about experiences with people you're close to, and in both, you were doing something a little mischievous. *It seems like* closeness and playfulness are important to you in your relationships, and *if that's the case*, I encourage you to keep using your school assignments as opportunities to explore these parts of your life." Regardless of whether they've met your expectations, saying back what seems important to them can help students clarify their values and find new ways to enact them.

Offering Suggestions for Growth

What could the student do to continue developing in ways that matter to that student and the community? Feedback on students' work would not be complete without suggestions for what to do the next time they have a similar assignment. What should they keep doing (because it was effective)? What should they start doing that would be more effective? What strategies, tools, and techniques would help them grow?

In making these suggestions, we can still honor the student's values. As Zohar's teacher, I might say, "I saw that the tree font mimicked the forest atmosphere of your camping trip, but it also made the poem itself hard to read. In the future, if you use a font that relates to a topic or theme, try using it just for the title. That way, you'll get your idea across without distracting the reader from the writing itself."

Rather than sending the message that their actions were bad or wrong, we can offer students ways to meet our expectations while also expressing their values. If they try those actions the next time they have a similar assignment, they'll learn that their values are not in conflict with academic standards and that it's possible to act on multiple sets of values at once.

In addition to suggesting what students can do in their work, you can encourage them to explore the work of real-world practitioners in your discipline who have similar values to theirs. When I saw Zohar's interest in conveying ideas both visually and verbally, I suggested that she read poems that have been turned into children's books and graphic novels. When another student wrote about his great-grandparents surviving the Holocaust, I recommended reading Jennifer Roy's *Yellow Star* (2006) and reaching out to the author. Telling students about people who have expertise on topics that matter to them, places in the community where they could learn more, and relevant media resources helps them discover mentors and role models within your discipline.

You could also suggest ways for students to do what matters to them outside your class and discipline. For example, if a student turns a chemistry assignment into a political cartoon, the teacher could suggest submitting political cartoons to the local newspaper or hosting a political artmaking event. Even if the student doesn't take these suggestions, they might be more attuned to future opportunities to act on their values. It also helps the student feel appreciated and respected—not only for what they do in your class but also for who they are in the world.

Finding Our Common Humanity

When I think back on the day I got zero points for the "million things" assignment, I used to wish teacher-me could travel back in time to give 5th-grade-me a hug. I imagined telling her that she'd grow up to become a teacher who helps students collaborate rather than compete, gets excited when they come up with unexpected approaches to assignments, and tries every day to make every student feel included and important.

Now I also wish teacher-me could travel back in time to give Mrs. Rivkin a hug. Here was a teacher who was trying to get students excited about a new topic. She gave assignments that fostered exploration and problem-solving. She had high expectations, and she wanted to motivate students to develop positive learning behaviors. Maybe she defined success too narrowly and shouldn't have used extrinsic rewards or created a competition for who was most successful; she instead should have helped students experience the vitality and satisfaction that come with doing meaningful work and building authentic relationships. Still, she was working hard to create an environment in which students would engage.

According to her LinkedIn profile, Mrs. Rivkin (remember, that's not her real name) started teaching in 1983. When she taught me, she was only three years into a teaching career that would last more than three decades. In 2013, a local magazine named Mrs. Rivkin "Top Teacher." (It's not Top Banana, but it's the same idea.) In the article about her, a parent described Mrs. Rivkin's impressive ability to understand each child, and Mrs. Rivkin said that our job as educators is to foster a love of learning and help kids discover their gifts.

I remember so little from 5th grade beyond that episode with the million points, but maybe Mrs. Rivkin did see me after all—or maybe she learned over time how to see students for who they were and honor the values they brought to their work. Either way, we've probably all gotten so stuck in our own definitions of success that we've lost sight of our students' experiences. I know I have. The best we can do is acknowledge our mistakes, hold ourselves accountable, and honor the humanity we share with our students.

Onward

This chapter was about how we can honor students' definitions of success without sacrificing our own. We can think of assessment as an ongoing conversation that helps students bring their strengths and values to their work. In the next chapter, we'll move from how students can connect to their work to how they can connect to each other. We'll see how academic learning is an ideal context for students to build meaningful relationships with one another and develop an authentic learning community.

PART

III

• • •

Engaging with Each Other

8

Respectful Discussions

I taught at a school where the behavioral code was based on respect for one-self, others, and the environment. Respecting oneself consisted of actions such as arriving on time and completing assignments, but respecting others and the environment consisted of *inactions* such as not disrupting class, not harassing people, and not defacing school property. Our behavior code might have sounded community-oriented with two out of three prongs looking beyond the self, but students' only responsibility to their peers and surroundings was to leave them alone.

I'm not calling out my former school in particular. Every school I've encountered defines respect through inactions. Students come to school to receive an education and are responsible for doing the required work satisfactorily, but their responsibilities to each other and their environment go no further than in any other transactional situation. People who go to the same movie theater or shop at the same grocery store follow certain rules so as not to infringe on one another—again, through inactions such as not talking during the movie or not cutting the checkout line. Beyond this noninterference, they have no responsibilities to their fellow customers. Most schools expect the same of students.

Respect doesn't have to mean getting out of each other's way. It can mean finding a way toward each other—and making a way forward together, as a community.

Many schools create community-building programs such as advisory, peer mentoring, affinity groups, field days, and overnight trips. Some teachers carve out time during their classes for community-building activities such as icebreakers, check-ins, movement breaks, and holiday celebrations. At their best, these activities and programs help students feel understood, recognized, and supported.

However, if community building only occurs outside the academic classroom, students get the message that community itself has nothing to do with academic learning. They often have trouble taking community building seriously when the serious business of school—academics—exists in an entirely separate domain, especially when that domain is individualistic and competitive. Meanwhile, the academic classroom is an ideal context for a sense of community to emerge. Students in the same class already have a shared identity ("who we are"—members of that class), a shared purpose ("why we're here"—to learn the course material), and an important collective endeavor ("what we do"—meaningful work).

If we want our classrooms to become communities, then we need to do more than make rules that keep students from interfering with one another's learning. We need to structure the learning environment so students actively make each other feel seen, heard, affirmed, recognized for their strengths, and supported in their struggles as they all strive to do what matters to them.

A good opportunity to begin transforming classrooms into learning communities is when students have discussions. In this chapter, we'll see what actively respectful discussions entail, what kinds of behaviors typical class discussions promote, and how to structure class discussions so students show active respect to each other.

Features of Actively Respectful Discussions

Try the following writing exercise.

1. Think of a specific time you participated in a discussion that felt actively respectful. That is, the participants understood, recognized,

and supported one another. Describe the situation. Where were you? Whom were you with? What was the discussion about? What did people do to show they understood, recognized, and supported one another?

2. Think of a specific time you participated in a discussion that did *not* feel actively respectful. That is, the participants did not seem to understand, recognize, or support one another. Describe the situation. Where were you? Whom were you with? What was the discussion about? What did people do that indicated they did *not* understand, recognize, or support one another?

3. Think of a specific time you participated in a discussion in which other people actively respected one another but not you. That is, the participants seemed to understand, recognize, and support each other but did not extend that understanding, recognition, and supportiveness to you. Describe the situation. Where were you? Whom were you with? What was the discussion about? What did people do to show they understood, recognized, and supported one another but not you?

4. Based on your responses to the first three prompts, what does it mean to engage in an actively respectful discussion?

I'll start with a time when people respected each other but not me. It was during a party conversation when the topic of C-sections came up. As it happened, my child was born by C-section three months prior. Also in the conversation were Donnie, who was present when his child was born by C-section six months prior, and Britt, who was in the OB/GYN rotation of her training as a physician's assistant. It could have been a great discussion because each of us had a different perspective, but every time I tried to say something, Donnie or Britt talked over me. The few times I managed to get a word in, they responded with "Yeah" and resumed talking to each other. They even physically faced each other and closed me out. Despite my being the only one in our little group who'd actually given birth by C-section, the other two people were utterly uninterested in my experiences. Even though it was 15 years ago, I still remember that day because of how unwelcome and insignificant they made me feel.

By contrast, a discussion I had that was actively respectful was with my friend Taslim. She and I were cocreating a virtual workshop, and we both felt dissatisfied with how things were going. After some self-reflection, I realized I was used to presenting alone, and when I'd cofacilitated, my colleague and I had divided the time and done our own parts. When Tas and I talked, I explained that history and apologized for making assumptions about how we would work together. She listened, asked questions to make sure she understood me, and validated my experiences even though hers had been different. We both agreed that as excited as we had been about our workshop, the process of our working together was more important—and our friendship was most important.

As for a discussion in which people did not actively understand, recognize, and support one another? Once, a friend who joined my family for a holiday meal observed that we all talked at the same time, but when my father spoke, all other conversation stopped. The talking at the same time part didn't bother me; as New York Jews, we used a communication style called cooperative overlapping (Tannen, 1994), which isn't considered rude and in fact conveys mutual interest and shared memory. What bothered me is that we'd all stop to listen in reverence to a man, and not to any of the women, nonbinary people, or children. Other than when we all listened to my dad, we talked in groups of two or three, thus excluding anyone who couldn't hear over the din of several simultaneous conversations. Meanwhile, the same few people monopolized every conversation to prove how much they knew.

These examples reflect discussions with my family, friends, and old acquaintances. Students participating in a class discussion have a different purpose and different relationships. Nevertheless, the examples might help us identify features of an actively respectful discussion:

- **Participants reflect before they contribute.** This could simply mean people think before they speak, or they might use a method that fosters deeper reflection, such as journaling or annotating a text. Reflection, even when it's just an occasional brief pause to consider one's words and their potential impact, helps participants make the discussion safe and satisfying for everyone.

- **Participants contribute and listen equitably.** This doesn't mean everyone must take the same number of turns or talk for the same number of minutes. It means each person makes a meaningful contribution according to their knowledge and strengths, and each person listens to everyone else in a way that makes them feel seen and heard.

- **Participants respond supportively to one another's contributions.** Support doesn't mean agreement. Depending on the circumstances, we might support a fellow participant by noticing what matters to them, asking questions to show we take their ideas seriously and are curious to know more, sharing insights or goals the discussion inspired, expressing our genuine emotions, showing empathy for someone else, or asking to continue the discussion in the future. Everyone has a basic need for belonging and esteem (Maslow, 1943; Tay & Diener, 2011). Responding supportively to another person's contributions ensures their belonging and esteem needs are met.

Keeping these features of an actively respectful discussion in mind, let's turn to how class discussions are typically structured and whether those discussion structures promote active respect.

Traditional Class Discussions

In a traditional class discussion, the teacher asks a question, hands go up, the teacher calls on a student, and that student answers the question. Some students share whatever comes to mind and think aloud in front of their peers. By the time other students decide what they want to say, the discussion has moved on. Even teachers who pause after asking a question don't always wait long enough for students to craft a thoughtful response.

Traditional class discussions don't ensure equitable participation. Some teachers track who's spoken and how many times, but if only five students raise their hands throughout the discussion, they're the only ones who contribute. If the five hand-raisers are white, male, cisgender, able-bodied, or neurotypical, then those voices are the only ones in the discussion. A well-intentioned teacher might call on marginalized students who aren't raising their hands, in effect asking those students to represent their sociocultural groups instead of treating them as individuals and compelling them to contribute when everyone else gets to choose.

Finally, in a traditional class discussion, students might not listen to one another except to determine whether their own responses are still worth sharing. Imagine that Riley's teacher asks why so many cities are located near water. Riley thinks it's to make travel easier. She raises her hand, but the teacher calls on someone else who says it's so the people have water to drink. Riley puts her hand down, thinking perhaps her answer was wrong. The teacher says, "People do need a source of drinking water, but many large cities are built near salt water, and you can't drink that." Riley's hand shoots back up because she thinks her answer might be the one the teacher wants. She doesn't engage her classmate (for example, by wondering if coastal communities are less drought-prone); she listens to her peers only to compare her own response to theirs.

Ultimately, a traditional class discussion is hardly a discussion at all when participants mostly interact with a central authority figure and not each other.

Alternative Discussion Formats

Seeking more inclusive and interactive discussions, many teachers use alternative formats such as turn-and-talks, seminars, and fishbowls. Unfortunately, these formats present many of the same problems as traditional class discussions. In a turn-and-talk, instead of one student talking at a time, everyone turns and talks to a partner. Although this structure creates more opportunities for students to contribute, any pair might have one student who does most of the talking, and even when both students talk, they don't necessarily have a meaningful interchange. The first student talks while the second student waits, then the second student talks while the first student waits, then both students wait for the rest of their class to finish talking. As the name suggests, a turn-and-*talk* involves speaking but not always listening.

In seminars, students do listen to each other. The teacher (or a student) poses a question, usually about a text. A student responds to the question, and then everyone keeps the discussion going. They can agree or disagree with one another, offer additional evidence to support someone's point, share a new perspective, or ask a new question. Seminars foster inquiry and interchange, but the discussion unfolds so rapidly that even if students have a chance to prepare responses to the initial question, they don't necessarily have a chance to consider how they'll respond to one another. Moreover, the seminar structure doesn't prevent a student from dominating. Some teachers track who talks and who doesn't, but then students end up jockeying for airtime so they get a good grade or become so anxious about *how much* they're saying that they focus less on *what* they're saying. Tracking who speaks doesn't account for how useful those contributions are, let alone how well students listen to each other.

Fishbowl discussions are a lot like seminars but with an inner ring of discussants and an outer ring of students who observe. Because the inner ring contains fewer people (say, half the class instead of everyone), each student has more opportunities to talk, but nothing ensures they contribute equitably or recognize one another's contributions as important. After the discussion ends, students in the outer ring give feedback, but if one student dominates, everyone might focus on that person (with admiration or criticism), and other students might not get much recognition for whatever they've managed to say.

These alternative formats increase active participation, but they don't necessarily increase active respect. Some students might be considerate toward their classmates, and teachers might encourage undercontributors and discourage overcontributors, but the formats themselves don't ensure students reflect before contributing, participate equitably, or respond supportively to one another.

Establishing Discussion Norms

Another way teachers attempt to make discussions actively respectful is by establishing discussion norms. The teacher might ask, "What do you need from the group in order to do your best in a discussion?" or "What do we need to do during discussions so this is a safe and productive learning environment?"

or simply "How will we have discussions in this class?" Students then generate a list of respectful behaviors such as these:

- Listen attentively.
- Contribute but don't dominate.
- Question assumptions.
- Use evidence when making a claim.
- Use *I* statements when describing your own experiences.
- Take responsibility for your own harmful actions. Apologize, make a repair, and do better in the future.
- Interrupt other people's harmful actions.

After negotiating which behaviors are most important and how to phrase them, the class agrees to abide by the norms they've established. Norm-setting helps students determine expectations instead of simply following the teacher's rules. Students reflect on their own needs and hear their classmates' needs, which can evoke self-awareness and empathy. A group's norms indicate their shared values and purpose, which helps build a sense of community.

We often learn group norms implicitly, just by being in a particular group. For example, no one ever explained cooperative overlapping to me or told me to do it; I learned by hearing my family use it. I also learned—without wanting to—to stop and listen to men when they speak. Making norms explicit helps students more intentionally choose behaviors that match their values.

Moreover, if discussion participants come from diverse backgrounds and therefore have learned diverse norms, making the group's norms explicit reduces the likelihood of cross-cultural misunderstanding. For example, if you grew up with the discussion norm that one person talks while everyone else remains silent, you might find me rude if I start talking before you finish. However, because I grew up with cooperative overlap as a discussion norm, I might read your silence as apathy. Working together to create norms for their class discussions helps students understand each other and experience each other as understanding—although the group's discussion norms can easily reproduce dominant cultural modalities.

Establishing norms makes everyone responsible for monitoring behavior. It's important for students to be aware of how their actions affect others and hold themselves accountable, and academic discussions are a great context to learn those skills. At the same time, whatever attention they devote to monitoring their behavior does *not* go toward the discussion's content.

Staging Discussions to Promote Active Respect

Once we consider how students need to divide their attention, we might realize that an actively respectful discussion is not one task, but many:

- Developing meaningful responses to the initial discussion prompt.
- Selecting parts of their responses that would be most helpful to contribute.
- Knowing when it's their turn to make their contribution.
- Making sense of their classmates' contributions.
- Developing meaningful responses to their classmates' contributions.
- Deciding which responses are worth sharing.
- Sharing their responses.
- Synthesizing meaning from the overall discussion.

Do we really expect students not only to complete all these tasks but also to decide from moment to moment which one to focus on? That's a lot to demand of anyone but especially of students who have varying levels of interest in the topic they're discussing, confidence in themselves, comfort in the group, and skill in managing their behaviors.

Furthermore, we don't always ask students to do all these tasks—let alone teach students how to perform them. Without explicit guidance and dedicated time to do otherwise, students typically prioritize responding to the teacher's prompt (because that's how they achieve academic status or the relief of being finished) at the expense of listening to, learning from, and validating one another.

If we separate the discussion into its component tasks, we can explain how to complete each one as it comes up, rather than overwhelming students with instructions and rules. Although the fact that there are eight different tasks might feel intimidating at first, some take only a minute or two. When we dedicate time to each task before moving on, we can ensure equitable participation at every stage, and students can devote their full attention to making meaningful contributions and to understanding, recognizing, and supporting one another as fellow members of the learning community.

Student Task #1: Respond to a Series of Writing Prompts

Ideally, these are prompts that have no right answer and instead create opportunities for students to explore the material, look for patterns, develop interpretations, tell stories, and imagine possibilities. For students to have a meaningful discussion, each of them needs to bring a meaningful contribution to it.

Let's go back to the geography class studying why cities tend to be built near certain physical features. Imagine that the teacher gives the following prompts:

- Which four physical features would you least want to live on? Draw four comic panels showing why you'd hate living on each of these features.
- Look at the physical world map showing the world's 15 largest cities. What can you say about all of them? Most of them? Some of them? One or two of them? None of them?
- What can happen in a coastal city that can't happen, or can't happen as easily, in an inland city?

These prompts give Riley more ways to interact with the content—and therefore more to share in a discussion—than one question about why so many cities are located near water, and she'll still end up exploring that concept. Chapter 2 offers much more guidance on how to write prompts that help students connect to the content and say something meaningful about it.

Three prompts give students enough different ways to say something meaningful about the content without overwhelming them. Allowing a few minutes for them to respond to each prompt before giving the next one means students can focus on the prompt in front of them, even if it's challenging. When I give the second and third prompts, I tell students that if they're still writing, they can keep writing, and the next prompt is there when they're ready for it.

By writing their responses, students get their thoughts into the physical world where they can observe them. Writing enables students to focus on and really listen to their own thoughts before they share with and listen to each other.

Student Task #2: Read Over Everything They Wrote and Mark Off a Portion They're Willing to Share

Instead of having an answer she isn't sure is correct, Riley has lots of writing and drawing from which she can select a portion that she thinks would be especially worthwhile for her classmates to hear. Because she has a sense of humor, she's excited to share her cartoon about why she'd hate living on a bog, butte, geyser, or glacier.

I usually ask students to mark off a *substantial* portion to share. If they ask for a minimum number of sentences, I encourage them to think about units of meaning instead. I say, "How much of what you wrote do your classmates need to hear in order to understand your idea?"

Sometimes, I ask students to notice any emotional changes as they read what they wrote. Any emotion—perhaps excitement about their phrasing, frustration over struggling to convey an idea, sadness as they consider implications, or joy as they relive a memory—means something important is at stake. That might be a part of their writing worth sharing, but even if they don't feel ready to, it's worth noticing for themselves.

Student Task #3: Establish a Sharing Order

When students know the sharing order in advance, they can listen to each other without constantly wondering when their turn will come. If Riley knows when she's sharing, whether it's third or twelfth or twenty-seventh, she doesn't have to keep raising her hand and wondering if and when her teacher will call on her; she can then listen more fully to what her classmates share.

Establishing a sharing order in advance also means you won't have to interrupt after every turn to say who will share next. When the first student finishes, that's the next student's cue to start. As a result, the only voices are the students', and the only topic talked about is the one they're discussing.

The easiest way to establish a sharing order is to seat students in a circle, ask for a volunteer to share first, and determine a direction (clockwise or counterclockwise). If your room won't accommodate a circle, or if your students don't do well in a circle, you can write an order on the board. I put numbered dot stickers on my students' desks so they have an order for whenever they share.

Student Task #4: Take Turns Sharing, and While Each Classmate Shares, Write Down the Sharer's Name and Some Nugget of What That Person Says

Some students struggle to pay attention during a share-out—either because they're uninterested in what a particular person says or because they're *so* interested that they get distracted by their own thoughts and stop listening. Here, as students listen to each of their classmates, they have something to listen *for* (a nugget they find meaningful) and something to *do* with the thing they heard (write it down); therefore, they remain attentive as everyone shares.

For example, as each of Riley's classmates shares, she writes down that person's name and a nugget of what they say, which helps her listen to everyone instead of zoning out. When it's her turn to share, she knows each of her classmates is writing down her name and a little nugget of what she says about bogs, buttes, geysers, and glaciers. She also has a chance to spell her name for her classmates so they know it's not Reilly or Rylee.

Writing down each person's name transforms the function of note-taking from merely recording information to attributing ideas to another person. As a student, I took classes where I didn't know my classmates' names. We were there to extract knowledge from the teacher, and perhaps from each other, but we didn't need to know each other's names to do that. Knowing their classmates' names, writing them down, spelling them correctly, and associating ideas with a fellow human helps students bring their whole selves to the classroom.

As for the nuggets students write down—recall that each student selected a particular portion they felt was important to share. As students listen to each other, they write down language or thoughts that, for whatever reason, *they* find important. By the end of the share-out, every student has written down everyone else's name and for each classmate, an idea both students find important. Having those mutually important ideas written down validates every person in the room and creates connections, however small, between every pair of students.

Student Task #5: Look Over Their Notes and Mark Anything They Want to Respond to

Just as they reconsidered their own responses to decide what to share, students now reconsider their classmates' responses to decide which ones they want to respond to. For example, Riley might have written down a lot of funny nuggets from her classmates' responses, but as she looks over her notes, she finds herself wanting to respond to more serious insights, so those are the ones she marks.

I usually tell students to choose whichever nuggets they're drawn to, but sometimes I ask them to notice any emotional changes as they read through their notes. For example, they might feel surprised by one classmate's point or grateful that another classmate raised an issue they were afraid to raise themselves. Emotions mean something important is at stake, and they might want to tell the group about it.

Student Task #6: Establish a Format for Responding to One Another's Contributions

The simplest format is to have students do another go-around, starting with the same person and moving in the same order as before, with each student responding to one classmate. You could change who goes first, change directions, or have students respond to two or three classmates instead of just one.

Another format is to pick someone to go first, have that student share a response to a classmate's contribution, and then have the respondee become the next responder. Because this process could continue indefinitely, you'll need to decide when to stop. Not every student will necessarily get a response, but those who shared larger portions of their writing, and those whose initial contributions went deeper or were more creative, will be more likely to garner responses from their classmates. If you use this format regularly, students who want to be recognized will learn to write more, share more, and take bigger risks. In addition, students will often keep track of who has already been recognized and deliberately include classmates who haven't.

Yet another format is to have students write the responses they most want to share on sticky notes, then walk around the room and stick their notes on one another's desks. This way, students can share as many responses as they want, and they'll get a sense of how big an impact their initial contribution made based on how many responses they get and what the responses say.

Student Task #7: When Responding to a Classmate, Say Back What that Person Said and Then Add Something of Their Own

Maybe Riley heard a classmate say that cities located near water can trade with one another more easily. When it's her turn to respond, Riley says that back and adds that she hadn't thought about trade because she was imagining people traveling from one place to another but that trade could be the reason for that travel. This type of responding allows Riley to appreciate her classmate's insight without feeling like hers was incorrect.

Saying back what a classmate said shows that person they were heard. Students might say back a direct quotation, which helps the person know their words had an impact, or they might paraphrase what their classmate said, which helps the person see how their words were interpreted. Either way, saying back what a classmate said validates that contribution.

After saying back what their classmate said, students add their own comment to show the impact their classmate had on them. Consider having your class brainstorm ways to do this, or give out a list such as the one in Figure 8.1.

Student Task #8: Discover Overarching Themes or Common Values that Emerged From the Discussion

It's often difficult for students to notice overarching themes and common values that emerge from a discussion when they're participating in it, so I recommend keeping track of these yourself so you can share them. You can either ask students to share themes and values they noticed, then add others you noticed, or share the themes and values you noticed, then ask your students if you missed anything.

FIGURE 8.1
Say Back and Add

Say Back and Add is a method of responding to other participants in a discussion.

First, say back something the other person said. If you directly quote them, they'll know exactly which of their words had an impact. If you paraphrase them, they'll know how you interpreted their words.

Next, add something on. Here are some ways to add on:

• Describe images that come to mind.

• Tell a related story. (Be brief so you don't take too much time or redirect attention from your classmate to yourself.)

• Ask a question. (Your classmate might or might not answer the question; the point is for *you* to show what you wondered.)

• Share an idea or a goal your classmate inspired.

• Say why you want to amplify that person's message.

• Explain how your classmate's perspective expands your thinking.

• Express an emotion.

• Express empathy.

• Connect your classmate's response to other responses in the group.

Other ways to add on to something a classmate says:

•

•

•

This last step is a good opportunity for you to amplify certain ideas and give a preview of future topics in the unit. For example, the geography teacher might reiterate the point about coastal cities being able to trade, then say that the next class will be about how trade routes and cities evolved together.

Pointing out common values can build community among students and help you design future lessons. When the geography teacher says many students seem to care about bringing their creativity and humor to their work, Riley feels seen as an individual while also experiencing a sense of belonging in the group. Meanwhile, the teacher realizes he wants more of his prompts to tap into his students' creativity and humor.

You might also choose to participate in the entire discussion process: write responses to your own prompts, select a part to share with your students, note something each student says, and offer responses. You can be strategic about what you share (for example, if you want to make sure a particular point comes up) and whom you respond to (for example, if there's a student whose contributions are undervalued in the group).

Structurally Respectful Discussions in Pairs and Small Groups

We've now seen how to use the actively respectful discussion structure with a whole class, but it works well for partner discussions and fishbowls, too—with a few modifications. For a fishbowl, only those students who are in the inner circle share portions of what they wrote (Task #4) and respond to their classmates (Task #7). Although students in the outer circle spend most of their time silently observing, they can still respond to the writing prompts (Task #1) and write nuggets of what students in the inner circle say (Task #4). They can also share any overarching themes or common values they noticed (thus being the ones to perform Task #8 instead of you).

When your class has partner discussions, you give only one writing prompt (Task #1) before asking students to consider whether they want to share everything they wrote or only part (Task #2) and decide which partner will share first (Task #3). Partner A shares while partner B writes down as many nuggets as they find important; then they switch roles (Task #4). Each partner individually decides which nuggets they want to respond to

(Task #5), and the two partners decide together whether they want to take turns again or have a more free-flowing conversation (Task #6). Either way, they use the say-back-and-add method to respond to each other (Task #7). It's difficult to share overarching themes and common values (Task #8) when many discussions occur at the same time, but you might pick up on certain recurring topics or insights, which you can name. You can also acknowledge the fact that you've prioritized deeper conversations, and more time for each person to share, over finding throughlines.

To be clear, I'm not saying you should use this structure every time your students have a discussion. It all depends on your goal. If your only goal for the discussion is to help students better understand the topic, then a traditional class discussion or a basic turn-and-talk often works just fine. If your goal is for students to learn discussion skills, then you might consider having your students experiment with various formats (including fishbowls and seminars) and explore how their ways of participating affect the discussion itself, their understanding of the subject matter, and the group's cohesion. A unit on discussion skills could benefit students, but unless you teach an English or communications course (and even if you do), such a unit might not fit in with the rest of your content. However, if your goal is to use discussions of any content as an opportunity for students to build an actively respectful learning community, you'll need to structure those discussions so they do.

Onward

This chapter was about how to structure discussions so students don't just avoid interfering with one another but contribute mindfully, participate equitably, and listen attentively so they can understand, recognize, and support one another. Class discussions thus become opportunities for students to build a learning community in the process of doing something meaningful together. However, discussions aren't the only opportunities for students to connect with each other. In the next chapter, we'll see how collaboration—working together to formulate an idea, solve a problem, or create a product—is another context in which students can develop positive relationships and a sense of belonging.

9

Collaboration Protocols

As an English teacher, I wanted my students to write about topics that mattered to them and develop their own writer voices, which mostly meant working individually. However, I did assign the occasional group project. The most successful was when, after watching various spoken-word videos and analyzing how the poets convey what's important to them, students worked in groups to compose and perform original spoken-word poems.

For that project, Nella, Esther, and Annie created a poem about their experiences with sexist microaggressions. They weren't friends and had very different lives, but sexism affected them all. Each student contributed her experiences and language to the poem, and together they shaped it into a cohesive whole. During their performance, each student solo-narrated segments about her own experiences, but their three voices united for lines that expressed their collective anger and demanded change.

Nella, Esther, and Annie knew from their classmates' reactions (and mine) that they'd created something special and important. They toured the school, performing their poem for the principal, their other teachers, their friends, and random people in the hallway. They performed their poem at a school assembly. Three years later, as high schoolers, they performed their poem on International Women's Day, revising it slightly to explicitly include Black, Indigenous, Asian, Latina, and trans women. Throughout the writing process, they really listened to each other. They took each other seriously. They argued, but they did so in the service of creating something they all wanted to be as good as possible, and they made each other feel heard. They became friends.

When a collaboration goes well, each student draws from their individual knowledge and skills for a collective benefit. Students have an opportunity to produce a higher quality work product, find more satisfaction in the work process, and develop meaningful relationships. They also practice interpersonal skills they'll need in their workplaces, such as remaining open to new ideas, listening, asserting themselves, showing empathy, giving and accepting support, holding themselves and others accountable, resolving conflicts, and sharing credit for success.

That's when collaboration goes well, but as most of us learn from experience, it often doesn't. Collaborating can produce work that represents everyone's strengths, or it can produce work that represents the lowest common denominator. It can be a deeply satisfying process, or it can be frustrating and involve bickering, domineering, free-riding, and fooling around. Collaborating can create relationships or destroy them. Given all that can go wrong in a group, we can't simply tell students to work together and hope for the best. We need to structure collaborations to maximize the benefits and minimize the drawbacks.

We also need to recognize that collaboration does not only mean a group project. Students can also engage in collaborative inquiry, where together with a partner or small group, they make observations, tell stories, ask questions, find patterns, analyze problems, and invent solutions. Project-based collaborations involve creating a product or performance, whereas inquiry-based collaborations involve creating understandings or ideas.

This chapter is about how collaborative projects and inquiries present different kinds of problems and how we can use protocols to structure both types so they lead to an excellent work product, a satisfying work process, and positive working relationships.

Project-Based Collaboration

Projects enable students to use their learning, make an impact, share their voices, and enact their values. Group projects enable students to build on one another's learning, amplify their impact, join their voices together, enact their shared values, and build relationships in the process. With these benefits come three major challenges:

- **Collective decision making.** Unlike individual projects, for which students can make all decisions themselves, group projects require everyone to agree. Some students struggle to set aside ideas they're passionate about, relinquish creative control, and make compromises. Others struggle to express an opinion when caught between two arguing peers. When working on a group project, students need to make decisions together.

- **Equitable workload distribution.** In individual projects, students have only themselves to hold responsible for completing all the work, on time, to their own standards. In groups, each student does part of the work, and they're all responsible to each other. Sometimes, a student simply doesn't do their part, which leaves their groupmates either to do it themselves (thus taking on more than their fair share of labor) or to have it undone (thus ending up with an incomplete product or performance). Other times, different students have different work processes, standards, and timelines. A student who prefers to do his work right away might feel frustrated if his partner mulls her ideas over and completes the work closer to the deadline. She might find his work sloppy, though, so she redoes his part and feels resentful. During group projects, students need to distribute the workload equitably.

- **Compassionate communication.** Most projects have many interlocking parts and multiple stages of work. Group members need to be in constant communication with one another so they know about each new development in the product ("I ended up writing two paragraphs instead of one") and process ("It's taking me longer to collect data than I expected"). However, students sometimes feel embarrassed to admit their struggles and ask for help, or they might be so used to working alone that they don't check in with each other when they make decisions. All this might lead students to fight, blame each other for problems, complain about each other, or insist a groupmate's actions are "fine" when they clearly aren't. Students in a group need to communicate compassionately with themselves and one another so they can recognize their own setbacks, support one another, problem solve together, resolve conflicts, and recommit to a common purpose.

Any project requires significant time and effort, and it results in a product that will be seen and judged. Despite the adage that many hands make light work, group projects require even more work from students as they navigate the inherent relational challenges. Understanding this, some teachers engineer group projects to lighten the relational workload. For example, a teacher might

- Assign topics so students don't have to decide on one themselves.
- Subdivide the work product so each student is responsible for one part (in which case their work is not so much a group project as an assemblage of individual projects).
- Sign off on each step in the work process before students move on.
- Make final decisions for groups when they argue.
- Split up groups that are having conflict.

These measures help students focus on completing the project itself, and sometimes they're necessary. However, every time we tell our students what they *should* do, we take away an opportunity for them to notice what they *could* do and make a choice, together, based on the work and relationships they want to create.

Although students might struggle to make decisions collectively, divide their work equitably, and communicate compassionately, engaging in those challenges is precisely how they derive the benefits of collaborating. Instead of engineering the project to lighten the relational workload, we can provide protocols that enable students to do that work themselves.

Relational Protocols for Collaborative Projects

Protocols give groups step-by-step guidelines for interacting so they can achieve their shared purpose in accordance with their shared values. Some students dislike protocols, preferring more spontaneous interactions—especially when they're in a small group. According to education professor Joseph McDonald and his colleagues (2015), protocols feel "artificial to most novice users—a function of the constraints they impose" (p. 3) but that "under the right circumstances, constraints are liberating" (p. 1). By constraining interactions, protocols liberate the group from behavior patterns, power dynamics, and individual agendas that can frustrate the group's purpose and subvert shared values.

The relational protocols that follow give students clear guidelines for interacting when they're working on a group project so they make decisions collectively, distribute work equitably, and communicate compassionately.

Topic Appraisal

When we ask a group to pick a topic for a project, they can usually come up with *something*—but not necessarily something everyone in the group finds meaningful. Some groups might think they've reached consensus if no one expresses disagreement. Some groups vote, but that can leave dissenters working with a topic they don't find interesting or important. A student with higher social status might bend everyone else to their will. I've even seen students annoy each other into submission. Some of these topic selection methods are fairer than others, but they can all result in students feeling dissatisfied with their topic, which isn't a great way to begin a collaboration.

Rather than putting students into groups that select a topic together, this protocol has students form groups based on topics of mutual interest.

When to Use: before any significant group project

Suggested Time: 20 minutes

Materials: writing supplies

Protocol Steps:

1. Explain the project, including the fact that students will work in groups. You may wish to hand out an assignment statement, rubric, and exemplars so students fully understand what their groups will create.

2. Ask students to privately list potential topics for the project.

3. Invite volunteers to suggest topics they think would lend themselves especially well to the project and write these topics on the board. Figure out how many groups there will be, and aim for about twice as many suggested topics.

4. Ask each student to write their name on a sheet of scrap paper, copy all the suggested topics onto the paper, and rate how they feel about each one. They should use the following rating scale:

     5: excited

     4: interested

     3: willing

     2: hesitant

     1: opposed

5. Invite students to write explanations of why they feel the way they do about any topic.

6. Collect the papers. Let the class know you can't make any promises but you'll do your best to create workgroups based on topics students prefer.

Sometimes, a student expresses a compelling reason to work with a topic no one else rates highly. Imagine that Dominique recently learned that her ancestors lived in Ghana, and she's started reading about Ghanaian culture. Her math class is doing a project for which groups plan a travel itinerary and budget, and she wants to do Ghana, but no one else gave it a high rating.

In a case like this, you have several options. You could simply give the student their second choice, but that risks marginalizing a student who already has unique interests or circumstances. You could talk up the topic to other students, but if they say they'll work with it, you won't know if they're genuinely interested or if they feel they have to say yes to please their teacher. (Friendly, open-minded students often get tapped for favors, and they should get to work with their preferred topics, too.) You could offer the student the option of working alone, but then you're asking them to choose between a topic they care about and getting to work with their peers. If they choose to work alone, then other students might ask if they, too, can work alone, and the students who most need to practice their collaborative skills are often the very ones who want to work by themselves.

Working in a group means balancing individual and collective interests. You can name that for your students, letting them know you want them to do projects that matter to them *and* experience the benefits of collaboration. After you place students into their groups, make their first task together to share what about the topic interests them, how the topic might be challenging to work with, and why their future self will be glad they engaged with this topic. The topic brings the group together; talking about why it matters helps students begin to connect with one another.

Committed Action Protocol

Psychologists Steven Hayes, Kirk Strosahl, and Kelly Wilson (2012) define a *committed action* as "a values-based action that occurs at a particular moment in time and that is deliberately linked to creating a pattern of action that serves the value" (p. 328). They characterize committed action as an always available choice; people can choose to live by their values every day, rechoose to live by their values after they inevitably stray, and build a pattern of choosing to live by their values over time. Committed actions are

- **Specific:** We can recognize exactly what we're doing that feels important.
- **Concrete:** We can see, hear, and feel the results of the actions.
- **Positive:** We're doing something, not avoiding doing something.
- **Diverse:** We can live by our chosen values in many possible ways.
- **Vitalizing:** Although the actions might not feel comfortable or pleasant in the moment, they make us feel more fully alive.

This protocol helps students work together to choose committed actions as a group. It helps students not only establish behavioral expectations but also link those behaviors to values they want to live by. Committed actions represent not how they've been told they *should* behave while collaborating but how they *choose* to approach their work and each other, based on what matters to them. Their actions while working on a group project become part of building a life they find meaningful.

When to Use: at the beginning of any significant group project

Suggested Time: 45 minutes

Materials: Group Actions chart (Figure 9.1) for each group, Values in Groups handout (Figure 9.2) for each group, writing supplies

Protocol Steps:

1. Ask the class, "When things go well, what's great about working in a group?" Encourage them to draw from their own experiences and observations of groups that worked especially well together. As students share the benefits of working in a group, write their suggestions on the board.

2. Ask the class, "What can be terrible about group work?" Again, encourage them to draw from their experiences and observations. As students share the drawbacks of working in a group, write their suggestions on the board.

3. Have students get into their groups.

4. Distribute the Group Actions chart (Figure 9.1). Point out the prompts in the first column: "During group projects, we love it when . . ." and "During group projects, we hate it when . . ."

5. Within their groups, students pass the chart from person to person, each writing one thing that can happen during group projects that they especially love (for example, "During group projects, we love it when people think of ideas together") and explaining their thinking to the group. Then they pass the chart around a second time, each writing one thing they especially hate (for example, "During group projects, we hate it when people don't do their share of the work") and again explaining their thinking. Students can use the lists you wrote on the board to guide them, but they can also change the language or add something new. There should be no repeated statements;

FIGURE 9.1
Group Actions

During group projects, we love it when . . .							

During group projects, we hate it when . . .							

FIGURE 9.2

Values in Groups

Accuracy	Efficiency	Imagination	Reasonableness
Ambitiousness	Enthusiasm	Inclusivity	Reliability
Appreciation	Equity	Independence	Respect
Authenticity	Fairness	Interdependence	Responsibility
Carefulness	Flexibility	Involvement	Seriousness
Clarity	Forgiveness	Kindness	Sophistication
Compassion	Freedom	Knowledge	Straightforwardness
Connection	Generosity	Open-mindedness	Supportiveness
Consideration	Grace	Optimism	Sustainability
Courage	Gratitude	Organization	Thoroughness
Creativity	Harmony	Patience	Transparency
Curiosity	Honesty	Peace	Trustworthiness
Decisiveness	Honor	Persistence	Unity
Depth	Hope	Playfulness	Warmth
Diversity	Humor	Productivity	Wisdom

a student who'd planned to say something that was already said should select a different thing they love or hate about group projects.

6. Explain that loving or hating a particular action tells us something important is at stake. The stronger we feel, the more important that something is. Have students label the second column of the Group Actions chart "because we care about . . ." As they do, distribute copies of the Values in Groups handout (Figure 9.2).

7. Explain that *values* are qualities we think are important to bring to our actions. Students might be so used to framing their behaviors as achieving status (high grades, popularity) or avoiding unpleasant consequences (embarrassment, detention) that they struggle to think of their behaviors in terms of values. The values listed in the handout are qualities people can bring to their actions and interactions in groups.

8. Groups work together to fill out the second column, using the Values in Groups handout to guide them. Students might write more than one value in any particular box, and they can repeat the same value

in multiple boxes. They should fill out the second column so they're extending the sentences they started in the first column. For example, they might write, "During group projects, we love it when *people think of ideas together* because we care about *creativity*" or "During group projects, we hate it when *people don't do their share of the work* because we care about *equity and responsibility.*"

9. Ask students to peak-fold their charts along the dashed line (so the first column is folded back) and place the papers down in front of them so they can only see the other two columns. Explain that the values they identified as important to them can guide what they do in their groups. With that in mind, have them label the third column *"we will . . ."* and consider what they will do in their groups, based on what they care about.

10. Students work together to fill out the third column with actions they can choose to take while working on their group project, in accordance with the values they identified. Tell students to make their actions specific, concrete, positive, diverse, and vitalizing— explaining these terms as needed. In particular, explain that a *positive* action involves doing, not avoiding. For example, if a group wrote that they hate it when people interrupt each other, they might be tempted to write that they will *not* interrupt each other. That's not an action; it's the absence of an action. A positive action might be "take turns speaking" or "give each other a chance to finish our thoughts before we respond." Students should fill out the third column so they're extending sentences that begin in the second column. For example, they might write, "Because we care about *creativity*, we will *talk about our ideas instead of just going with the first idea*" or "Because we care about *equity and responsibility*, we will *split up the work fairly, set deadlines, and meet them.*"

11. Invite each group to share their committed actions. They should read them as complete sentences: "Because we care about ____, we will ____." Sharing their committed action plans with other groups helps students support one another's work and discover more ways they can choose to live by their values.

By the end of this protocol, each group will have generated a list of actions they can choose to take, in accordance with their values. However, the real work isn't stating the commitments; it's keeping them, which is what the next protocol is about.

Accountability Check-In

Nobody acts in accordance with their values all the time. Accountability means noticing when we break our commitments and then recommitting to our values. Psychology professor Kelly Wilson asks, "In that moment, the moment in which we notice that we're out of alignment with one of our values, can we pause, notice our dislocation, and gently return? It's difficult to imagine a value of any magnitude that will not involve a lifetime of gentle returns. This turning back makes all the difference" (Wilson & DuFrene, 2010, p. 133).

This simple protocol helps groups take that pause to observe their actions and notice whether they're in alignment with their values. They celebrate successes, apologize to themselves and one another for failures, and renew their commitment to their collective values.

When to Use: at the end of every work period during a group project (or every work period when you can make the time)

Suggested Time: 5 minutes

Materials: a copy of the group commitments drafted during the Committed Action protocol

Protocol Steps:

1. Group members sit so they're all facing one another.
2. One person reads the group commitments out loud to make them more present.
3. Students take turns responding to the following prompts while the rest of the group listens in silence:

    — Which commitments did I keep today?

    — Which ones did I struggle to keep today?

    — Why are those actions important to me personally?

— What will I do next time to recommit?

— Have I done any harm that I need to apologize for?

— What can I do to repair the harm?

If students use this protocol to close each work period, they remind themselves they can always recommit to their values. Often, when students choose behaviors that match their values, they end up with a better product or performance. Even if they don't, recommitting to their values makes the work more inherently satisfying and creates a sense of community.

Inquiry-Based Collaboration

In an inquiry-based collaboration, students work together to explore the content. Together, they observe, describe, remember, imagine, interpret, categorize, critique, wonder, experiment, and play. They're not cocreating a product or performance; they're cocreating *meaning*. An inquiry group might produce something tangible, such as a list or diagram, but their work is not so much to bring that thing into existence as to discover truths and possibilities through the process of making it. A project can be finished, but inquiry is perpetually unfinished.

Due to its nonfinality, an inquiry tends to have lower stakes than a project. When students do a project, the teacher uses its outcome (the product or performance) as evidence to assess what students know and can do. Each individual's participation affects the entire group's success. By contrast, an inquiry has no predefined outcome; the outcome is the process itself. The teacher can assess how students approach that process as individuals, and one student's participation won't make or break another's successful learning. Therefore, students in an inquiry group don't have to rely on each other to the same degree as in a project, which means they don't have the same types of relational challenges. They can simply engage in the inquiry together and build relationships along the way.

That said, if students are working together on something they just as easily could do alone, they might feel like the group just slows them down. Perhaps you've seen someone race ahead on a task they were supposed to do with a group—or perhaps you've been that person. When my 8th grade math teacher had us work on practice problems in groups, I was the kid who plowed through the whole page by myself and then doodled or wrote poems while the rest of my group was still working. My groupmates had every right to be annoyed, but I honestly don't think they cared. I felt a little guilty—but not guilty enough to slow myself down and work with the group.

However, in history class, I had the opposite problem. I struggled to make sense of the readings, so when we got a set of questions to answer in groups, I had nothing to offer. I was the kid everyone else waited for while I wrote down somebody else's answer before the group could move on. It was pretty humiliating.

Although I experienced my math and history assignments differently (and I'm sure my groups experienced *me* differently), they were structured in the same way: as a set of separate tasks. Each math problem and history question was its own undertaking, unrelated to the others in the set. In a group, students could do each task together, but that means taking the time to explain their thinking and make sure everyone understands. More often, when groups get a set of separate tasks, they split up the work and exchange answers. That's a sensible approach if the goal is simply to get the work done as quickly as possible, but exchanging answers doesn't deepen learning or relationships.

If our goal is for students to build relationships in the process of engaging in meaningful inquiry together, we need to structure the inquiry task so the work is reciprocal and synergistic. When work is reciprocal, everyone contributes something meaningful to the group and gains something meaningful from the group. One example of a task that is structured for reciprocity is the jigsaw: each student learns individually about a particular subtopic and then shares their knowledge with the group, thus adding a piece to the puzzle. Imagine that a science class is learning about unicellular organisms. The teacher places students into groups of three; one studies the amoeba, one studies the paramecium, and one studies the euglena. Each student then teaches the other two what they learned, so now all three students know about all three organisms.

In a jigsaw, everyone contributes knowledge to the group, and everyone gains knowledge from the group. The task is reciprocal but not synergistic.

That is, the outcome is merely the sum of its component parts. When a task is synergistic, the group creates an idea that is somehow more than the sum of its parts. When a task is both reciprocal and synergistic, students make something together that can only exist because of what they each contribute and how the group transforms those ingredients.

Activity Protocols for Collaborative Inquiry

The following protocols structure collaborative inquiry to be both reciprocal and synergistic. Everyone contributes something to the group and gains something from the group, and the group develops something that is more than the sum of the individual contributions. In the process, students build relationships with each other.

Distinguish and Define

In many units of study, students deepen their knowledge of a concept they already know something about. This protocol helps students articulate their current understanding so they can build on it. First, students distinguish a concept (such as *rivers*) from a related concept (such as *bodies of water*). Then they come together in groups to define the concept. Finally, the whole class comes together to share and refine their definitions.

When to Use: early in a unit, when students access their existing knowledge about the unit topic

Suggested Time: 25 minutes

Materials: writing or drawing supplies

Teacher Preparation:

1. Create a series of writing or drawing prompts that ask individual students to represent a concept they'll study, along with one or more associated concepts. Figure 9.3 shows example prompts asking students to represent concepts in various subjects.

2. Create a discussion prompt that will help groups use their writing or drawings to help them collectively define the concept. Figure 9.3 has examples of discussion prompts that help students define the concepts together, based on the writing or drawing they did individually.

FIGURE 9.3

Example Prompts for the Distinguish and Define Protocol

	Rivers	Data Representations	Phoniness in *The Catcher in the Rye*	Belonging
Writing or Drawing Prompts: Individuals represent a unit concept along with one or more associated concepts.	• Draw a river. • Draw two bodies of water that aren't rivers.	• Take a bag of pretzels. Make a graph that clearly represents the nutrition information. • Make a different kind of graph that clearly represents the nutrition information. • Make a third graph that represents the nutrition information in a way that is misleading.	• Make a list of people or things Holden considers phony. • Make a list of people or things Holden *doesn't* consider phony.	• Describe a time when you felt like you were part of a community. • Describe a time when you were in a group that did not feel like a community. • Describe a time when you were in a community but felt like you didn't belong.
Discussion Prompts: Groups use their writing or drawings to collectively define the unit concept.	• Based on everyone's drawings, what is a river?	• How can data representations help people make decisions? • How can they mislead people into making decisions that don't serve them?	• Based on what Holden does and doesn't consider to be phony, how is he defining *phoniness*? • Is he a phony according to his own definition?	• Based on what you wrote and heard, what does it mean to belong to a community?

Protocol Steps:

1. Give a series of writing or drawing prompts that help students distinguish a concept they're studying from one or more associated concepts. Share one prompt at a time so students can fully attend to each one instead of rushing through one response to get to another. Have students write or draw their responses individually and silently.

2. Break the class into groups of three or four.

3. Give groups a discussion prompt that helps them develop a common definition or understanding of the concept, based on what they all wrote or drew.

4. Invite groups to share their definitions or understandings with the whole class. Write their suggestions on the board.

5. Lead the class in attempting to combine the groups' definitions or understandings into one consensus definition or understanding they can all use as they move forward in the inquiry.

Words-Images-Annotations-Relationships

When students read a text, they encounter important new terms. This protocol has students explore key terms using various expressive modalities. There are several rounds, during which students offer their own perspectives, negotiate meaning within small groups, and learn from other groups. At the end, the class assembles their work so they can see interrelationships and patterns. Together, they turn a list of keywords into a network of meaning.

Because this protocol has a long title, I abbreviate it as WIAR. You can pronounce WIAR as "why are," which is appropriate for an inquiry, or as "we are," which is appropriate for a collaboration.

When to Use: in the middle of a unit, when students encounter key terms they need to understand

Suggested Time: 45 minutes

Materials: for each group: one sheet of unlined paper, one black marker, one set of colored pencils or crayons, one black pen, one 4×6 index card, tape

Teacher Preparation:

1. Gather the materials.

2. Identify key terms in an assigned reading. Although students will identify key terms themselves as part of the protocol, you may wish to already have a sense of which terms will be most important for them to explore in groups.

    — Example terms about the breakup of Yugoslavia: *power vacuum, nationalism, balkanization, secession, annexation*

    — Example terms about wetlands: *transition, habitat, absorb, degradation, conservation, restoration*

    — Example terms about graphing lines: *axis, point, slope, intercept, parallel, perpendicular, intersecting*

3. Have students do the reading, in class or for homework, before they begin the protocol.

Protocol Steps:

1. Break the class into groups of two or three.

2. Lead the class in brainstorming important words or phrases from the reading, and write these terms on the board. Be sure students brainstorm enough terms that each group will have a different one.

3. Distribute the materials. Explain that during this activity, students will explore the terms in several different ways, using different materials at each stage. At the end of each stage, they'll pass their paper to another group and receive another group's paper, which they'll then work on. Create a passing pattern and make sure each group knows which group they'll pass papers to and which group they'll receive papers from.

4. Assign one term to each group.

5. Instruct each group to use a black marker to write their assigned term across the full sheet of paper so the word's look fits its meaning. Students might consider whether the letters should be capital or lowercase, soft or hard, spiky or curly, filled in with a pattern, and so on.

6. Each group passes their paper to the next group and receives a paper (with a word) another group worked on.

7. Tell groups to use crayons or colored pencils to draw images that convey the word's meaning. They should not use any labels or captions—only images.

8. Each group passes their paper to the next group and receives a paper (now with an illustrated word) two other groups have worked on.

9. Tell groups to use a black pen to annotate the images. They should explain how the images illustrate the term and add any information or analysis that would help someone understand the term's meaning.

10. Collect all the papers and tape them to the wall so they form a circle, with space between the papers.

11. Assign each group a pair of terms that are next to each other in the circle.

12. Have groups describe how the two terms relate to each other. They should write these descriptions in pen on an index card.

13. Ask one person from each group to tape their card to the wall between the two relevant terms.

14. Lead a brief discussion using the following prompts:

    — What do you notice as you look at our completed work?

    — What did you notice as you worked on the pieces?

    — What ideas emerge from the completed work? What does it show us about [the unit topic or theme]?

Connections, Distinctions, and Absences

This protocol has students write about their experience of a text—what they thought, felt, remembered, wondered, guessed, or imagined as they read or viewed it. In groups, they discuss what their responses have in common, why they're different, and what none of them include. The course material becomes a context for each student to notice their own perspective ("I"), their peers' perspectives ("you"), their shared perspective ("we"), and the fact that they have a perspective.

When to Use: later in a unit, when the topic is more familiar and students are ready to go deeper

Suggested Time: 35 minutes

Materials: writing supplies

Teacher Preparation:

1. Choose a short, intellectually and emotionally stimulating text (such as a chapter, an article, a comic, a poem, a video, a photograph, a painting, a journal entry, or an essay) that will help students understand the unit content.

2. Create three writing prompts that elicit various ways of interacting with the text. The questions can invite students to observe, speculate, ask questions, imagine possibilities or impossibilities, take a position, solve a problem, tell a story, find a pattern, notice their physical or emotional reactions, or otherwise have a psychological response to the text or anything in it. (See Chapter 2 for further guidance on how to create prompts; the sections on deictic and exploratory prompts are especially relevant.)

3. Have students do the reading or viewing, in class or for homework, before they begin the protocol.

Protocol Steps:

1. Give three writing prompts that invite students to interact with the text in various ways. Share one prompt at a time so students can fully attend to each one instead of rushing through one response to get to another. Students write their responses individually and silently.

2. Break the class into groups of three or four.

3. Ask students to share their responses within their groups, looking for connections, distinctions, and absences. Use the following discussion prompts, or some version of them:

    — **Connections:** How were your responses similar in content (what you said) or approach (how you thought about the prompt)?

    — **Distinctions:** What differences stand out, and what might account for these differences?

— **Absences:** What didn't come up in any of your responses? What
haven't you experienced or thought about?

4. Bring the class back together for a brief share-out. Ask the following
questions:

— How was that?

— What did you discover?

Continuum of Understanding

When students encounter challenging material, they sometimes make
extreme statements such as "This makes *no* sense" or "I don't get this *at
all.*" Nevertheless, they might understand certain aspects, make sense of
things they didn't understand at first, and find that things they thought
they understood become less clear.

Although students usually think of understanding as *good* and a lack
of understanding as therefore *bad*, perplexity and doubt are normal and
expected features of learning (and, I'd say, of being human). During this
protocol, students recognize their own varying degrees of understanding
and then respond to one another with validation, clarification, more questions, a different perspective, or other forms of support.

When to Use: whenever students encounter especially challenging material

Suggested Time: 40 minutes

Materials: copies of the Continuum of Understanding chart (Figure 9.4),
writing supplies

Teacher Preparation:

1. Make copies of the Continuum of Understanding chart (Figure 9.4).

2. Have students read, view, or otherwise encounter challenging material,
in class or for homework, before they begin the protocol.

Protocol Steps:

1. Break the class into groups of four or five. Each group should sit in
a circle.

2. Distribute copies of the Continuum of Understanding chart (Figure 9.4) and instruct students to fill out the topic and their initial
thoughts. Have them do this individually and silently.

FIGURE 9.4
Continuum of Understanding

Topic:				
Initial thoughts:	I understand . . .	I'm guessing	I'm unsure about . . .	I have no idea about . . .
	How I know:	Why I think that:	My questions:	My needs:
Responder 1:				
Responder 2:				
New thoughts:				

3. Ask students to pass their papers to the right. Have them write their name where it says "Responder 1" and silently respond to what their classmate wrote in each column. They might

— Validate a classmate's reaction.

— Explain something to a classmate.

— Clarify something for a classmate.

— Thank their classmate for clearing up their confusion.

— Answer one of their classmate's questions.

— Ask more questions of their own.

— Offer a different perspective.

— Celebrate a shared understanding.

— Commiserate in shared confusion.

4. Ask students to pass the papers again. Have them write their name where it says "Responder 2" and respond to the initial thoughts at the top, build on what Responder 1 said, or do a combination.

5. Ask students to pass the papers back to the original writer. Have students write their thoughts about anything they see in the various responses.

6. At this point, students have interacted with each of their groupmates as either a responder or a respondee (or both), but they haven't yet talked as a group. Ask students to discuss their thoughts in their groups.

7. Lead a brief share-out about the content and process, using the following prompts:

— How was that? How did it feel to do this work together?

— What were some of the interesting moments in your written or spoken discussions?

— What lingering questions do you have?

Find and Sort

Some material is more complex than it seems. For this protocol, students work in groups to find many specific examples of a larger concept, sort their examples into categories, and share their categories with other groups. As they build their conceptual understanding, they more fully appreciate the topic's complexity, the diverse ways information can be sorted, and the diverse minds in the room.

When to Use: whenever students encounter material that is more complex than it might first appear

Suggested Time: 40 minutes

Materials: enough packs of sticky notes in two different colors that every group will have one pack in each color, writing supplies

Teacher Preparation:

1. Choose a topic or theme you want students to explore in greater depth, and for which they'll be easily able to find many different examples. Sample topics and themes (in various subjects and grade levels) include

   — Reflexive verbs in Spanish

   — Chesapeake Bay wildlife

   — Units of measurement

   — Multivariable equations

   — Harlem Renaissance artists

   — Cold War figures

   — Protest methods used during the civil right movement

   — Ways the pigs use their power in Chapters 6 and 7 of *Animal Farm*

   — Things Holden Caulfield says about Sally in Chapter 17 of *The Catcher in the Rye*

   — Healthy breakfast recipes

   — Warm-up exercises

   — Biased headlines

2. Gather materials, including the sticky notes and any resources that will help students find lots of examples.

Protocol Steps:

1. Break students into groups of three or four.
2. Give each group one pack of sticky notes, along with any other resources they might need to help them find examples of the topic or theme.

3. Ask groups to find *lots* of examples of the topic or theme and write each example on its own sticky note.

4. Give each group another pack of sticky notes, which can be any color other than the one they've already used.

5. Instruct each group to sort their examples into categories, using sticky notes from their new pack to label the categories and arranging all the sticky notes so everything they wrote is visible and it's clear which items belong to which category. Students should have at least two categories, and there should be no categories with only one example. They are allowed to add examples after they've thought of their categories.

6. Have students walk around the room, visiting the other groups' tables to see what examples they found and how they sorted them.

7. Lead a whole-class discussion, using the following prompts:

   — What did you notice as you sorted your examples?

   — What did you notice as you looked at other groups' examples and categories? Did anything surprise you or stand out?

   — How did this activity help you understand [the activity topic]?

   — How might this enhanced understanding of [the activity topic] help us as we continue to learn about [the overall unit topic]?

Each of these protocols helps students understand the material more fully and deeply. They contribute their ideas to the group, gain new ideas from the group, and create meaning as a group. In the process, they get to know themselves and each other, find affinities and honor diversities, and set themselves up to proceed in their inquiry as a learning community.

Onward

This chapter was about how to structure collaborations so an academic task becomes a context for students to build authentic and positive relationships. As they engage in projects or inquiries together, students come to appreciate their own strengths, their classmates' strengths, and the impact they make on each other's learning. The next chapter is about how students can develop and express that appreciation.

10

Appreciative Reflection

In 6th grade, we did an activity our teacher called a "compliment circle." Every week, she'd randomly choose one of our names, that person sat on a special spinning chair, and the rest of us pulled our regular chairs into a circle around them. The person in the middle turned to face us one by one, and each of us had to say something positive about them.

There were no guidelines besides "give the person a compliment," so some kids said things like "I like your shirt" or "You have a nice pencil case." Even when the compliments were about the person and not their belongings, they were usually pretty vague: "You're kind," "You're funny," and so on. Still, I loved the compliment circle. I loved the time I got to be in the middle, but I also loved getting to say things about my classmates and hearing what other people said about them. My heart pounded as the person in the middle turned their chair more and more toward me. I always tried to think of something substantive to say without repeating someone else.

The compliment circle was one of the very few times I can remember a teacher asking my class to appreciate each other. Maybe that's why, during journal time one day, I tore a page from my notebook and scribbled a message thanking everyone for being my friends and saying I was going to give each of them "a small gift" to show my appreciation. I folded the paper over, gave it to the boy who sat behind me in class, and tried not to watch as the note traveled around the classroom.

I didn't have a plan for what the promised "small gift" could be, but now everyone was expecting something. I thought maybe I could decorate paper bags and fill them with the little treats sold at the front of the toy store: a high-bouncer, a glow-in-the-dark keychain, a sheet of stickers, a few pieces of bubble gum. I imagined making bags for each of my classmates. Even the boys who baited me and then snickered at my responses. Even the girls who said, "Can someone come with me to the bathroom?" and pretended not to hear when I volunteered. Even the kids I barely talked to.

That afternoon, I asked my mom to take me to the toy store. When I told her what I wanted to buy, she said it was nobody's birthday; we were too old to play with toys; and I didn't have any money, and if I did, I shouldn't waste it on "cheap junk." I was too embarrassed to tell her I'd already promised the gifts, and I couldn't have explained why because I didn't understand myself.

But I do now.

I was trying to appreciate the people in my class and get them to appreciate me. I was also trying to appreciate—and get them to appreciate—that we had relationships with one another, not necessarily as friends but as people who were learning and growing together. As a student, I didn't know how to express appreciation for my classmates with anything but empty compliments, cheap gifts, and promises I couldn't keep. However, as a teacher, I could help my students learn the skills I'd lacked.

Many teachers include reflection activities to help students take stock of their learning. If we've structured students' learning experiences so they connect with one another, then reflection activities are an ideal time for them to appreciate each other and the relationships they've built. Moreover, reflection is itself a form of meaningful learning, so when students engage in it together, they not only appreciate their community—they reinforce their sense of community.

This chapter explores how leading reflection exercises at various points in an academic unit can help students appreciate themselves, one another, their relationships, and the learning community.

Purposes of Reflection

Education professors David Boyd, Rosemary Keogh, and David Walker (2015) describe reflection as "time to catch up with ourselves" (p. 8). How can it be possible for *us* to catch up with *ourselves*? Aren't we right there with ourselves all the time?

Yes and no. Psychologist Steven Hayes (1995) distinguishes three dimensions of the self: the conceptualized self, the knowing self, and the transcendent self. The conceptualized self is the main character in the story of your life: the person you describe when someone asks you to tell them about yourself. Depending on the situation, you might talk about your background, roles and relationships, cultural identity, professional history, personal interests, or psychological patterns—to name only some examples. These are all parts of your conceptualized self.

If the conceptualized self is like a character, the knowing self is like the author who understands what's happening, chooses what happens next, and decides what it all means in the larger story. Reflection gives the knowing self a chance to catch up with the conceptualized self: to pause, notice our external and internal circumstances, choose what we do, and decide what our actions will mean in our lives.

For students, catching up with themselves might include

- **Consolidating understandings:** What do you now know? How are the things you've learned interconnected?
- **Evaluating actions:** What did you do? How did that work out for you?
- **Setting goals:** What do you want to know, be able to do, and achieve in the near and distant future?
- **Clarifying values:** What made this experience satisfying and dissatisfying? What qualities do you want to bring to your actions and interactions?
- **Choosing future actions:** How will you achieve your goals and live your values? How can you celebrate, replicate, and build on your successes? How can you overcome your struggles? What will you do first? If that action doesn't work out, what else might you try?

As educators, when we ask students reflection questions, we use the second person: What do *you* now know? What did *you* do? What qualities do *you* want to bring to *your* actions? Such questions evoke answers from the first-person perspective: *I* know how to solve multivariable equations. *I* made a study outline and did practice problems. *I* want to check *my* work thoroughly so *I* don't make careless mistakes.

Psychology professor Kelly Wilson and his students describe the self as a repertoire—a set of perspective-taking behaviors. A sense of self "is cultivated in a crucible of questions that share one common feature: they all involve the person asked to take the perspective of 'I.' The answers to all of the questions, implicitly or explicitly, begin with the word 'I'" (Wilson et al., 2012, p. 188). When we take the perspective *I*, we're building and maintaining a sense of self. We're *I*-ing. The conceptualized self is *I*, but the knowing self does the *I*-ing.

At school, students already engage in *I*-ing all the time. They say things like, "I'm good at math," "I'm bad at writing," "I love history," "I hate group projects," "I'm the only nonbinary kid in my class," and so on. Their sense of self can be negative, limited, rigid, and even inaccurate or dishonest. When we ask reflection questions that elicit positive, expansive, flexible, and realistic *I* statements, we help students develop a positive, expansive, flexible, and realistic sense of self.

As important as *I*-ing is, each student isn't just *I* but a part of *we*. If *I*-ing builds a sense of self, *we*-ing builds a sense of community. The reflection tools in this chapter elicit responses from the first-person singular (*I*) and plural (*we*) perspectives to help students appreciate themselves as individuals and as part of a group. The questions that elicit answers from the third-person (*she*, *he*, *they*) perspective help students appreciate their classmates' skills and strengths, their relationships with their classmates, and the impact they and their classmates have on one another. Reflection thus becomes an act of more fully appreciating themselves, one another, and their community.

Reflective Check-Ins at the End of a Class Period

After a discussion or inquiry-based activity, students need to reflect on what they just learned about the topic. When they're working on a project, they need to reflect on their progress, next steps, and (if it's a group project) the work distribution. After students reflect on *what* they learned or did that day, consider having them reflect on *how* they engaged in that learning or work—and with each other. A brief reflective check-in helps students understand how their actions and interactions affected them.

To begin a reflective check-in, try asking a general question such as "How was that?" or "What did you notice?" Sometimes, one part of the experience is so salient that students seem to forget everything else, so you might name each part of the activity. For example, you might ask, "How were the writing, sharing, and responding portions of this discussion for you?" or "What did you notice as you searched for examples of bias? As you sorted your examples into categories? As you looked at other groups' categories?"

You can also distinguish between what students noticed while they were working and when they look back on their work, such as by asking, "What did you notice as your group created your food web? What do you notice now?"

Broad, open-ended questions like "How was that?" or "What did you notice?" give students an opportunity to respond with whatever is most important to them. The problem is, they can also respond with . . . whatever. Students can answer "How was that?" with a one-word evaluation—good, boring, easy, confusing, weird—without engaging in much reflection at all. "What did you notice?" can elicit observations of just about anything: "I noticed that methane pollution is a big problem and no one ever talks about it." "I noticed all the signers of the Constitution were men." "I noticed the lizard on page 22 is smiling." "I noticed I was hungry."

I won't pretend I never allowed comments like these in my classroom (or that I never made them myself). At the same time, reflecting on our own actions and interactions makes us vulnerable, and if we don't directly ask our students to do that, many just won't. That's why, if I ask a general question to begin a reflective check-in, I quickly follow up with more specific questions about the process.

Figure 10.1 offers questions about various aspects of the learning or work process. These examples are here to help you see possibilities, not to limit you. Tweak the language or use the questions to help you think of your own.

FIGURE 10.1

Reflective Check-In Question Bank

Below is a list of possible questions you can ask to help students reflect on their actions and interactions on a particular day. Choose just one or two questions to ask at the end of an activity or work period. Asking the same questions on different days can help students see patterns over time, whereas asking different questions gives them opportunities to explore different aspects of their learning, work, and community.

General Questions to Begin Process Reflection

- How was that?
- What did you notice?

Questions to Help Students Reflect on Their Actions

- What was most interesting about today's work?
- Who went somewhere unexpected in your own thinking or work? How was that?
- What was most challenging for you today?
- Did you give up at any point? How did that feel at the time? How do you feel about it now?
- Did you un-give up at any point? How did that feel at the time? How do you feel about it now?
- Would you call today's work a success? How are you defining *success*? How else might you define *success*?
- Based on how things went today, how will you approach similar activities in the future?
- What did today's work help you discover (or rediscover) about yourself?

Questions to Help Students Reflect on Their Interactions

- What did the group help you discover?
- How was it to share your ideas?
- How was it to hear other people's ideas?
- If someone responded to your ideas, how did that feel? If no one responded to your ideas, how did that feel?
- Were there thoughts you wanted to express but didn't get a chance to? What did you do at that point? What can you do now?
- At any point, did you feel like you had to prove you were right? What did you do with that feeling?
- How does it feel to have done this work together?
- Who did work that you want to recognize?
- Who gave you feedback on your work-in-progress? What did that person help you understand?
- Who suggested a resource for you to use? How did that help you?
- Who suggested a strategy for you to try? How did that help you?
- How did your group decide who would do what?
- What are some things each of your groupmates did well?
- What are some behaviors you want to work on the next time you're in a group?

A reflective check-in shouldn't take much time or feel like a whole other activity. Think of it as a brief moment when students can catch up with themselves and one another. Ask just one or two (or at most three) questions, giving students just a minute or two to respond to each. You can call on a few students to share their responses to each question, have them all share in pairs, or ask them to write their responses in their notebooks or on slips you collect.

In any case, the goal of this check-in isn't so much for students to share their reflections as to have an opportunity to acknowledge that they had an experience, appreciate themselves and one another, and see that reflection itself merits their attention.

Reflection Exercises for the End of a Unit or Term

Many reflection exercises ask the question "What are you proud of?" Students deserve to feel proud of working to broaden their knowledge, build their skills, and create important products and performances—and that pride can motivate them to put forth more effort in the future.

In addition to pride, reflection can evoke a sense of humility. Humility is not the absence of pride; it's pride in context. It's seeing our triumphs and strengths while also seeing our stumbles and needs. It's seeing ourselves as important while also seeing others as important. Without diminishing our own accomplishments, humility means acknowledging how our relationships made our accomplishments possible—and how our accomplishments contribute to something larger and longer lasting than ourselves.

The following three exercises ask students to reflect with humility—pride in context—on their learning, work, and relationships during a unit. If you prefer, replace the word *unit* in any exercise with *term* or *semester* so students can reflect on that longer timespan. Unlike a reflective check-in, when students take just a few minutes at the end of class to notice themselves and each other, these end-of-unit exercises evoke deeper, more extensive awareness. The three different exercises offer students different entry points into appreciative reflection.

Appreciating Our Learning

This exercise asks students to notice and appreciate what they learned during a unit—not only about the topic but also about themselves as individuals and as a community.

Suggested Time: 15 minutes

Materials: writing supplies

Steps:

1. Lead your students in recapping the unit. You might ask them to look through their notes or take out a unit summary, syllabus, calendar, or study guide that could help them remember. As you and your students name major learning events, topics, assignments, and texts, list them on the board.

2. Ask the following questions, pausing after each so students have time to write a response.

   — During this unit, what are some things you learned how to do (or how to do better)?

   — During this unit, what are some things you learned about the topic?

   — During this unit, what are some things you learned (or relearned) about yourself?

   — During this unit, what are some things you learned (or relearned) about this learning community?

3. Give one final reflection prompt and ask students to respond in writing: "Imagine a future version of yourself—next month you, next year you, or maybe you several years from now when you've graduated and are an adult. Why will that future version of you be glad you know the things you've learned during this unit?"

4. Invite volunteers to share any of their reflections they think their classmates would benefit from hearing.

The first time you do this exercise, you might find that very few students share. You can encourage them by sharing first. What did *you* learn how to do, or how to do better, from teaching this unit? What did you learn about the topic from preparing lessons or from your students? What did you learn about yourself as you taught the unit? What did you learn about the learning community? Why will your future self be glad you learned all this? Sharing your responses to these questions might help students feel safer sharing. Even if they don't, they have an opportunity to appreciate their learning privately.

Appreciating Our Actions

Whereas the previous exercise had students reflect on the outcomes of engaging in a unit, this exercise has students reflect on what engagement means. First, they list actions they took during a unit or term. Then they evaluate their actions in two ways: how well they performed them and how much they enjoyed them. Finally, they appreciate ways they can do more of what they enjoy, find collaborators whose preferences complement their own, use their strengths to benefit their community, and draw on their community to address their weaknesses.

Suggested Time: 25 minutes

Materials: copies of the Action Graph (Figure 10.2), writing supplies

Steps:

1. Lead the class in brainstorming actions they've taken throughout a unit. As students come up with actions, write each one on the board as a phrase that begins with an *–ing* verb. The actions might be academic, relational, or managerial in nature. For example, actions during a unit on Latin American physical geography might include *locating* major physical features (academic), *discussing* how physical features influence cultural features (academic and relational), *selecting* physical features for a group artmaking project (relational), *dividing* the work (relational and managerial), and *maintaining* a project schedule (managerial). Students might need help remembering what they did during the unit, so consider asking them to look through their notes or take out a unit summary, syllabus, calendar, or study guide.

FIGURE 10.2
Action Graph

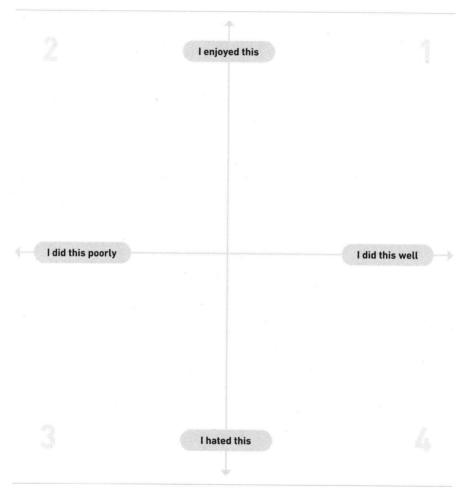

They might also need prompting to think of academic, relational, and managerial actions.

2. Distribute the Action Graph (Figure 10.2), which has students evaluate each action in two ways: how well or poorly they did it, and how much they enjoyed or hated it. Point out that students should not evaluate how much they generally enjoy these actions or how well they usually perform them; they should evaluate their actions in the specific context of the unit or term. Also point out that enjoyment is

subjective and skill is relative. Actions other people enjoy might not be fun for them, and they might find actions other people complain about to be very enjoyable. They might have done well given their current level of skill but imagine being able to do much better—and they might define *better* differently from how you do. Encourage them to evaluate their actions based on their authentic preferences and current capabilities.

3. Ask the following questions to help students interpret their graphs, pausing after each one so students have time to write a response.

— For actions you enjoyed and did well (quadrant 1): What are some other opportunities for you to do these kinds of things? If you're not aware of other opportunities, who can you ask? How can you make sure you enjoy these actions fully?

— For actions you enjoyed but did poorly (quadrant 2): Who in this room could practice with you? Who outside this room could serve as a mentor?

— For actions you did poorly and hated (quadrant 3): Who are some potential work partners who seem to enjoy these actions and are good at them? What would you bring to that partnership?

— For actions you hated but did well (quadrant 4): How could you use those skills to benefit your community? Even if you don't enjoy the action itself, how could it help you build relationships you do appreciate?

4. Invite students to share, without saying what they wrote, how it felt to think about their actions and one another in these ways. Sharing their actual responses would make them vulnerable. Their classmates might disagree with their assessments of how well or poorly they did, and they might tease them for enjoying or hating something. Publicly expressing interest in working with a particular peer might feel awkward for everyone involved. However, sharing how it felt to evaluate their actions and imagine possibilities can help them build community.

When students share how they felt as they reflected, they might express feelings of frustration or embarrassment from not being good at something.

If that happens, tell them they're in the exact right place to improve their skills and that if they feel upset they can't yet do something well, that's a sign that doing it well is important to them. When they're aware of what matters to them, they have a choice: Will they do what it takes to improve? How will they feel if they put forth that effort, even if it's frustrating or embarrassing? How will they feel if they *don't* put forth that effort?

Students might also say they felt uncomfortable naming their peers, even in the privacy of their notebooks. If you get that comment, resist any urge to make students feel more comfortable. Instead, ask them to notice their discomfort. Where might it come from? Why might it be worth feeling? What could happen if they're willing to feel uncomfortable asking a class-mate to work together? What happens if they don't? Questions such as these help students develop the willingness to feel uncomfortable in the service of their values—or, at the very least, to notice they have a choice between com-fort (on one side) and building their skills and relationships (on the other).

Appreciating Classmates' Contributions

Whereas the previous two exercises include some reflecting on other people's strengths that is the entire focus of this exercise. It requires the most humility, which might make students feel vulnerable but also gives it the most potential to evoke a sense of community.

Suggested Time: 20 minutes

Materials: copies of the Appreciating Classmates questionnaire (Figure 10.3), writing supplies

Steps:

1. Lead the class in brainstorming responses to the following ques-tions, writing their answers on the board. You might ask them to look through their notes or take out a unit summary, syllabus, calendar, or study guide to help them remember topics, tasks, and the product or performance they created.

    — What did you learn about during this unit? (Title this list *topics*.)

    — What did you do in order to learn? (Title this list *tasks*.)

    — What did you create in order to reinforce and demonstrate your learning? (Label this item *product* or *performance*.)

FIGURE 10.3
Appreciating Classmates

Reflecting on *what* we learned (topics) . . .

- Which classmates seem to understand these topics especially well?

- Which classmates helped you understand these topics? What did they do to help you?

- Which classmates gave you new ways of thinking about these topics? What did they say to expand your thinking?

Reflecting on *how* we learned (tasks) . . .

- Which classmates did these tasks especially skillfully? What are their skills?

- Which classmates helped you engage in these tasks? What did they do to help?

- Which classmates helped you improve at these tasks? What did they do to help?

Reflecting on what we created (a product or performance) . . .

- Which classmates' products or performances were especially good? How so?

- Which classmates helped you create or refine your product or performance? How did they help?

2. Explain that students will reflect on how their classmates positively affected their learning. Distribute copies of the Appreciating Classmates questionnaire (Figure 10.3).

3. Give students time to write their responses to the questions. As they do, encourage them to keep looking through their notes so they can remember certain discussions, activities, and work periods more fully. Encourage them to look around the room so they notice classmates who might have contributed to their learning but whose contributions might not come immediately to mind.

4. Lead a discussion to debrief the exercise, using whichever of the following prompts you think would be most useful for your students:

    — Without saying who you recognized for what, how did it feel to recognize your classmates in these ways?

    — Without saying what your answers were, which questions did you find it easiest and hardest to answer?

    — Why aren't we going to share our responses out loud right now? What problems can you imagine that causing?

    — Without saying who they are, can you think of certain people who only get recognized or praised for certain skills? What if those aren't the skills they want to be recognized for? Even if they are, how might it feel to only be recognized for certain skills?

    — How can we appreciate a person's contributions without reducing them to those contributions?

    — How can we recognize a wider range of strengths in each other?

    — Since we aren't going to share publicly, what are some ways you could express your appreciation to a classmate privately?

    — How can you show appreciation for your classmates other than by praising or thanking them? Praising and thanking aren't bad things to do, but are there other ways to demonstrate appreciation?

    — If you feel like you aren't getting recognition for the skills and strengths that matter to you, how can you ask for that recognition?

    — How do you feel about yourself as a result of appreciating other people?

Asking students to notice their own accomplishments helps them appreciate themselves, but we don't have to stop there. We can also help them appreciate what they contribute to the group, what they get from the group, the fact that there *is* a group, relationships they're building with individuals in the group, and relationships they're building with the group as a whole. Reflecting with humility in no way lowers them. On the contrary, it's uplifting to situate accomplishments that belong to them within a community where they belong.

Transcendent Selves and Communities

This chapter's reflection exercises help students appreciate their own actions, their peers' actions, and the fact that they're part of an interdependent learning community. Through *I-ing* and *we-ing*, students build a sense of who they are. Their knowing selves have a chance to catch up with their conceptualized selves—and to conceptualize who they want to become, both individually and together.

There's one more dimension of self: the transcendent self (Hayes, 1995). Your transcendent self is the continuous *you*, the perspective that exists and persists throughout your life. Even though your actions depend on where you are, who you're with, and how you feel, you're still you. Even though you've changed throughout your life, there is a you who has done all that changing.

Because the transcendent self is so hard to describe, psychologists use metaphors. If your emotions are like weather, always in flux, your transcendent self is like the sky (Harris, 2009). If your thoughts are like fall leaves floating on a stream, coming and going, your transcendent self is the stream (Hayes, Strosahl, & Wilson, 1999). If your experiences are like meals, sometimes familiar and sometimes new, sometimes appetizing and sometimes awful, your transcendent self is the plate (Porosoff & Weinstein, 2018). If the conceptualized self is the main character in the story of your life, and the knowing self is the author, then the transcendent self is the reader.

Regular reflection builds students' awareness that there *is* a transcendent self, an *I* that exists and persists. There's a life story they're living, writing, and reading all the time. What do they want that story to mean?

What will exist and persist when this brief chapter of the story—your class—is over? Who will your students choose to be?

What about the community? The school year will end. Your students' individual selves will continue, but their learning community, as it exists in your classroom, will not. Aware of this ephemerality, we might be tempted to focus only on the individual self that endures, but we might also see the ephemerality as a reason to honor the learning community while it exists. By participating in a learning community, each student becomes part of a collective story, *we*, that in turn becomes part of their individual stories, *I* and *I* and *I*. The learning community endures within each individual learner.

Maybe that kind of engagement is as important as engaging with the essay or the math problem. Maybe building a sense of self and community is what engagement is for.

Conclusion: Our Jobs and Our Work

We've now seen 10 elements of instructional design that help students engage authentically with the content, their work, and each other. Every lesson, assignment, and interaction becomes an opportunity for students to discover who they want to be and how they want to live, in and beyond our classrooms. When you create a learning environment in which students can authentically engage, authentic engagement itself can become a way of life for your students.

That all takes time and energy—from students and from you. I've tried to make your work a little easier by providing tools and strategies you can use as they are or adapt so they fit your subject and students. Still, it takes intellectual, emotional, relational, and sometimes even physical effort to teach in a way that fosters authentic engagement. Just as acting in accordance with their values is a choice for your students, it's also a choice for you—every moment of every class period, every lesson and assignment of every unit of every academic year. What will you choose? If you choose to act on the values you want to bring to your teaching, what will the cost be? What will be the cost if you don't?

You have more than enough to do in the job you have, but I've always seen a distinction between our jobs in education and our work as educators. I've held many different jobs in education, but my work as an educator has always been about making school a source of meaning, vitality, and community in students' lives—and in teachers' lives, too.

Maybe designing instruction so your students connect authentically with the content, their work, and each other isn't part of your job, but it's part of your work. Maybe developing a pedagogy of authentic engagement, on your own and with your colleagues, will make school a greater source of meaning, vitality, and community in your life, too.

References

Alexander, K. L. (2019). Mae Jemison. *National Women's History Museum*. www.womenshistory
.org/education-resources/biographies/mae-jemison

Barnes-Holmes, D., Hayes, S. C., & Dymond, S. (2001). Self and self-directed rules. In S. C.
Hayes, D. Barnes-Holmes, & B. Roche (Eds.), *Relational frame theory: A post-Skinnerian
account of human language and cognition* (pp. 119–139). Kluwer Academic/Plenum.

Bishop, R. S. (1990). Mirrors, windows, and sliding glass doors. *Perspectives: Choosing and
Using Books for the Classroom, 6*(3), ix–xi.

Boyd, D., Keogh, R., & Walker, D. (2015). *Reflection: Turning experience into learning*. Routledge.

Bright, A. (2016). The problem with story problems. *Rethinking Schools, 30*(4), 14–19. https://
rethinkingschools.org/articles/the-problem-with-story-problems

Cisneros, S. (1991). *The House on Mango Street*. Vintage.

Cobb, J. A. (1972). Relationship of discrete classroom behaviors to fourth-grade academic
achievement. *Journal of Educational Psychology, 63*(1), 74–80.

Crenshaw, K. (1989). Demarginalizing the intersection of race and sex: A black feminist
critique of antidiscrimination doctrine, feminist theory and antiracist politics. *University
of Chicago Legal Forum, 1989*(1), 139–167.

Eberle, R. F. (1972). Developing imagination through scamper. *Journal of Creative Behavior,
6*(3), 199–203.

Eberle, R. F. (2008). *Scamper: Creative games and activities for imagination development*.
Routledge.

Education Week. (2018). *Differentiating instruction: It's not as hard as you think.* https://youtu.be/h7-D3gi2lL8

Fluckiger, J. (2010). Single point rubric: A tool for responsible student self-assessment. *The Delta Kappa Gamma Bulletin, 76*(4), 18.

Gilbert, P. (2010). *The compassionate mind: A new approach to life's challenges.* New Harbinger.

Gonzalez, J. (2014). Know your terms: Anticipatory set. *Cult of Pedagogy.* www.cultofpedagogy.com/anticipatory-set

Gorski, P. (2019). Avoiding racial equity detours. *Educational Leadership, 76*(7), 56–61.

Hammond, Z. (2015). *Culturally responsive teaching and the brain: Promoting authentic engagement and rigor among culturally and linguistically diverse students.* Corwin.

Han, B. (2020). *The disappearance of rituals: A topology of the present* (D. Steuer, Trans.). Polity Press. (Original work published 2019).

Harris, R. (2009). *ACT made simple: An easy-to-read primer on acceptance and commitment therapy.* New Harbinger.

Hattie, J., & Timperley, H. (2007). The power of feedback. *Review of Educational Research, 77*(1), 81–112.

Hayes, S. C. (1995). Knowing selves. *The Behavior Therapist, 18,* 94–96.

Hayes, S. C., Barnes-Holmes, D., & Roche, B. (Eds.). (2001). *Relational frame theory: A post-Skinnerian account of human language and cognition.* Kluwer Academic/Plenum.

Hayes, S. C., Strosahl, K., & Wilson, K. G. (1999). *Acceptance and commitment therapy: An experiential approach to behavior change.* Guilford.

Hayes, S. C., Strosahl, K., & Wilson, K. G. (2012). *Acceptance and commitment therapy: The process and practice of mindful change* (2nd ed.). Guilford.

Hughes, L. (2002). Theme for English B. *Poetry Foundation.* www.poetryfoundation.org/poems/47880/theme-for-english-b. (Original work published 1949.)

Hunter, M. (1982). *Mastery teaching: Increasing instructional effectiveness in elementary, secondary schools, colleges and universities.* TIP Publications.

Inoue, A. B. (2019). *Labor-based grading contracts: Building equity and inclusion in the compassionate writing classroom.* WAC Clearinghouse.

Kimmerer, R. W. (2013). *Braiding sweetgrass: Indigenous wisdom, scientific knowledge and the teachings of plants.* Milkweed Editions.

Lahaderne, H. M. (1968). Attitudinal and intellectual correlates of attention: A study of four sixth-grade classrooms. *Journal of Educational Psychology, 59*(5), 320–324.

Landfill Harmonic (2013). *Landfill Harmonic Movie Teaser.* https://vimeo.com/52129103

Lee, E., Menkart, D., & Okazawa-Rey, M. (Eds.). (1998). *Beyond heroes and holidays: A practical guide to K–12 anti-racist, multicultural education and staff development.* Teaching for Change.

Lei, H., Cui, Y., & Zhou, W. (2018). Relationships between student engagement and academic achievement: A meta-analysis. *Social Behavior and Personality, 46*(3), 517–528.

Li, Y., & Lerner, R. M. (2011). Trajectories of school engagement during adolescence: Implications for grades, depression, delinquency, and substance use. *Developmental Psychology, 47*(1), 233–247.

Livingston, D. (2016). Lift off. *Harvard Graduate School of Education*. www.gse.harvard.edu /news/16/05/lift

Martin, E. (1991). The egg and the sperm: How science has constructed a romance based on stereotypical male-female roles. *Signs: Journal of Women in Culture and Society, 16*(3), 485–501.

Maslow, A. H. (1943). A theory of human motivation. *Psychological Review, 50*(4), 370.

McDonald, J. P., Mohr, N., Dichter, A., & McDonald, E. C. (2015). *The power of protocols: An educator's guide to better practice* (3rd ed.). Teachers College Press.

McHugh, L., Stewart, I., & Almada, P. (2019). *A contextual behavioral guide to the self.* Context Press.

Newmann, F. M. (1992). *Student engagement and achievement in American secondary schools.* Teachers College Press.

Nitko, A. J., & Brookhart, S. M. (2007). *Educational assessment of students* (5th ed.). Pearson Prentice Hall.

NPR. (2022). *Three books . . . : One theme, three great reads.* www.npr.org/series/three-books

O'Connell, C. (2021). *Wild rituals: 10 lessons animals can teach us about connection, community, and ourselves.* Chronicle Prism.

Oldways Preservation and Exchange Trust. (2009). Latin American diet pyramid. https:// oldwayspt.org/system/files/atoms/files/Latino_pyramid_flyer.pdf

Oldways Preservation and Exchange Trust. (2011). African heritage diet pyramid. https:// oldwayspt.org/system/files/atoms/files/AfricanDietPyramid_flyer.pdf

Oldways Preservation and Exchange Trust. (2018). Asian diet pyramid. https://oldwayspt .org/system/files/atoms/files/AsianDietPyramid_flyer.pdf

Paschen, E., & Raccah, D. (Eds.). (2010). *Poetry speaks who I am.* Sourcebooks.

Porosoff, L. (2020). *Teach meaningful: Tools to design the curriculum at your core.* Rowman & Littlefield.

Porosoff, L., & Weinstein, J. (2018). *EMPOWER your students: Tools to inspire a meaningful school experience.* Solution Tree.

Porosoff, L., & Weinstein, J. (2020). *Two-for-one teaching: Connecting instruction to student values.* Solution Tree.

Roy, J. R. (2006). *Yellow star.* Marshall Cavendish.

Simons, D. (2010). *Selective attention test.* www.youtube.com/watch?v=vJG698U2Mvo

Simons, D. J., & Chabris, C. F. (1999). Gorillas in our midst: Sustained inattentional blindness for dynamic events. *Perception, 28*(9), 1059–1074.

Skinner, E. A., Wellborn, J. G., & Connell, J. P. (1990). What it takes to do well in school and whether I've got it: A process model of perceived control and children's engagement and achievement in school. *Journal of Educational Psychology, 82*(1), 22–32.

Stone, N. (2020). Don't just read about racism—read stories about Black people living. *Cosmopolitan.* www.cosmopolitan.com/entertainment/books/a32770951/read-black -books-nic-stone

Talusan, L. (2022). *The identity-conscious educator: Building habits and skills for a more inclusive school.* Solution Tree.

Tannen, D. (1994). *Gender and discourse*. Oxford University Press.

Tay, L., & Diener, E. (2011). Needs and subjective well-being around the world. *Journal of Personality and Social Psychology, 101*(2), 354–365.

Truth, S. (1864). I sell the shadow to support the substance. *Library of Congress*. http://hdl.loc.gov/loc.rbc/lprbscsm.scsm0880

Varo, R. (1961). La llamada. *National Museum of Women in the Arts*. https://nmwa.org/art/collection/la-llamada-call

Villatte, M., Villatte, J. L., & Hayes, S. C. (2016). *Mastering the clinical conversation: Language as intervention*. Guilford.

Voerman, L., Korthagen, F. A., Meijer, P. C., & Simons, R. J. (2014). Feedback revisited: Adding perspectives based on positive psychology. Implications for theory and classroom practice. *Teaching and Teacher Education, 43*, 91–98.

Waltz, T. J., & Follette, W. C. (2009). Molar functional relations and clinical behavior analysis: Implications for assessment and treatment. *The Behavior Analyst, 32*(1), 51–68.

Wilson, K. G., Bordieri, M., Whiteman, K., & Slater, R. M. (2012). The self and mindfulness. In L. McHugh & I. Stewart (Eds.). *The self and perspective taking: Contributions and applications from modern behavioral science*. (pp. 181–198). Context Press.

Wilson, K. G., & DuFrene, T. (2009). *Mindfulness for two: An acceptance and commitment therapy approach to mindfulness in psychotherapy*. New Harbinger.

Wilson, K. G., & DuFrene, T. (2010). *Things might go terribly, horribly wrong: A guide to life liberated from anxiety*. New Harbinger.

Wisniewski, B., Zierer, K., & Hattie, J. (2020). The power of feedback revisited: A meta-analysis of educational feedback research. *Frontiers in Psychology, 10*, 3087.

Woo, E. (2018). How math is our real sixth sense. *TED Conferences*. www.ted.com/talks/eddie_woo_how_math_is_our_real_sixth_sense

Yoon, N. (2021). Black girls need their happily-ever-afters too. *Cosmopolitan*. www.cosmopolitan.com/entertainment/books/a36419641/nicola-yoon-black-joy-essay

Index

The letter *f* following a page number denotes a figure.

absences, acknowledging, 40
adulting, 67
agency, 66
assessment
    affirming assignments, 93*f*
    assignment evaluation tool, 93*f*
    collaboration, inquiry-based, 160
    honoring student values, 124–126
    inquiry groups, 160
    task choice, 71–73, 72*f*
assignments, affirming
    the audience in, 87–88
    designing, 85–89
    evaluation tool, 93*f*
    generating, 89, 90–91*f*, 92
    inquiry-driven units, 79–80
    neighborhood essay, 94–97
    products and performances, 79–80
    real-world resemblance for, 85–87, 96*f*
    rehearsal-driven units, 80
    relatability in, 88–89
    student viewpoint, 79–80
assignments, expectations and, 110. *See also*
    schoolwork
attention, selective, 115–117
audience in affirming assignments, 87–88

books. *See also* learning materials
    evocative, 38
    non-issue, 12
    prompts to situate in a larger
    conversation, 41–42

check-ins, reflective, 176–177, 178*f*, 179
choice, meaningful, 66–68
choice boards, 63, 64–66, 64*f*, 65*f*
classrooms as community, 132
collaboration
    inquiry-based, 160–162
    poetry project, 148–149
    project-based, 149, 150–152
    successful, 149
collaborative inquiry, activity protocols
    connections, distinctions, absences, 166–168
    continuum of understanding, 168, 169*f*, 170
    distinguish and define, 162, 163*f*, 164
    find and sort, 170–172
    words-images-annotations-relationships,
    164–166
collaborative projects, relational protocols
    for
    accountability check-in, 159–160
    committed action protocol, 154–155,
    157–159

Group Actions chart, 156*f*
topic appraisal, 152–154
Values in Groups handout, 157*f*
communication, compassionate, 150–151
community
    in authentic engagement, 3–4
    building, 132, 176
    classrooms as, 132
    ritual and, 45–46
    transcendent selves and, 187–188
compliment circle, 173–174
course content
    connective prompts in, 32
    deictic questions, 33–35, 35*f*, 36*f*, 37*f*
    deictic variations to connect to, 34–35
    evocative texts, 38
    exploratory prompts, 38–42
    meaning-finding/meaning-making, 36

decision making, collective, 150
deictic questions
    examples, 33–35, 35*f*, 36*f*
    meaning-finding/meaning-making, 36
    planning tool, 37*f*
deictic relations, 32–34
deictic variations, 34–35
details, collecting, 39
discussion
    alternate formates, 136–137
    respectful, 132–135, 139–147
    traditional, 135–137

empathy, 11
empowerment, 66
engagement, authentic
    characteristics, 2–4
    defining, 1–2
    purpose of, 3–4, 188
essays, personal, 94–95
exemplars, 102–105, 105*f*
expectations, sharing, 109–110
experiences, perspective in, 32–34

family conferences, 1–2
feedback
    evaluative, 110
    honoring students' humanity, 122–126
    responsive, 106, 107*f*, 108, 109*f*
    suggestions for growth, 125–126
find and sort, 170–172
fishbowl discussion, 137

girl, looking for the, 9–10
grading contracts, 64–66
Group Actions chart, 156*f*
group discussion, 146–147

group projects. *See* collaboration, project-based

#VoiceAndChoice, 66
hiking the blue trail, 27–28
humanity
    finding our common, 126–127
    honoring students,' 122–126
humility, reflection and, 179

I-here-now, 32–34
I-ing, 176
inclusivity. *See also* learning materials, inclusive
    intersectional, 12–14
    local and current, 14–15
inquiry groups. *See* collaboration, inquiry-based
interests, student
    connecting to, 29–30, 31*f*, 32, 38–39
    looking beyond, 32–34
intersectionality, 12–14

jigsaw, 161–162

learning materials
    books, evocative, 38
    evocative, 38
    non-issue, 12
    resource look, 50–51
learning materials, inclusive. *See also* learning materials
    choosing with self-reflection, 16–17, 16*f*
    functional analysis and replacements, 17–20
    looking for, 9–10
    making changes, 23–25
    as mirrors and windows, 10–12, 13, 15
    other than books, 15–16
    resource crowdsource protocol, 21–23
    resources for, 20–21
    selecting with reflection, 25*f*
learning tasks. *See* task choice
lesson, defined, 60

meaning, cocreating, 160
meaning-finding/meaning-making, 36
motivation, intrinsic, 80, 82
multimodal responses to prompts, 42, 44

neighborhood essay, 94–97

parent conferences, 1–2
perspective, 32–34
poetry assignment, 58–59
possibilities, prompts for imagining, 40–41

potential, celestial, 82–83
pride, 179
prompts, connective
    course content, 28–29, 32
    deictic relations, 32–34
    hiking the blue trail, 27–28
    rituals, 45–46
    student interests, 29–30, 31*f*, 32
prompts, exploratory
    acknowledging absences, 40
    collecting details, 39
    describe psychological experiences, 41
    eliciting student questions, 40
    examples, 43*f*
    imagining possibilities, 40–41
    multimodal responses, 42, 44
    purpose of, 38–39
    responding to, 42, 44
    situate the text in a larger conversation, 41–42
psychological experiences, describing, 41

questions, prompts for eliciting, 40

reading with empathy, 11
reflection
    appreciative, 173–174
    with humility, 179
    purposes of, 175–176
reflection exercises tor appreciation
    check-ins at the end of class, 176–177, 178*f*, 179
    classmates' contributions, 184, 185*f*, 186–187
    end of unit or term exercises, 179–187
    learning, 180–181
    our actions, 181–184, 182*f*
respect, defining, 131–132
rituals
    connective prompts and, 45–46
    function of, 45
    messages communicated, 45–46
    orienting, 45
    for transitioning, 46–57
rubrics
    example, 118*f*
    to express judgements of success, 123–126
    parallel, 118–122, 122*f*
    student-made, 119–120, 119*f*
    using for success, 117

Say Back and Add, 144, 145*f*
SCAMPER, 89, 90–91*f*, 92
schoolwork. *See also* assignments, affirming
    a real-world contribution, 79–80, 81*f*, 82
    as self-expression, 82–83

as selfing, 83–85
    student vs. teacher perspective, 78
self, the, 175–176, 187–188
self-expression, schoolwork as, 82–83
selfing, schoolwork as, 83–85
seminars, 136–137
service learning, 14–15
stimulus function transformation, 27–28
student interests, connective prompts and, 29–30, 31*f*, 32
success
    defining, 114–115
    expressing judgements of, 123–126
    humanity component in, 122–127
    noticing, selective attention and, 115–117
    Top Banana, 113–114
success, co-constructed definitions of
    feedback in, 122–126
    rubrics in, 117–123, 118*f*, 119*f*, 122*f*
success criteria, sharing, 110

task choice
    generating, 60–61
    limitations, 73–74
    meaningful, 66–68
    poetry assignment, 58–59
task choice, values-based
    fostering, 68–71
    selection protocol, 68–69
task choice assessment, 71–73, 72*f*
tasks
    brainstorming, 61*f*
    defined, 60
    equitable, 66–67
    expressive, 62, 63*f*
    generic examples of, 60
    receptive, 62, 63*f*
    student-created, 65–66
task variety
    benefits of, 61–62
    choice boards, 63, 64–66, 64*f*, 65*f*
Top Banana, 113–114
transitioning
    to a new unit, 47–51
    out of a unit, 54–57
    rituals in, 46–47
    between topics within a unit, 51–53
turn-and-talk discussion, 136

units of study
    anticipatory sets, 49
    clear-outs, 56–57
    defined, 47
    lesson titles, 52–53, 53*f*
    resource look, 50–51
    sensory experiences, 54–56

transitioning between topics within a, 51–53
transitioning out, 54–57
transitioning to a new, 47–51
values activation, 49–50, 50*f*
unit summaries, 48–49, 48*f*

Values in Groups handout, 157*f*

words-images-annotations-relationships, 164–166

work, creating meaningful
exemplars for, 102–105, 105*f*
neighborhood essay, 94–97
responsive feedback in, 106, 107*f*, 108, 109*f*
teaching the skills of, 97
topic selection process, 97–102, 99*f*
work process, staging the, 109–111, 111*f*, 112
workload distribution, equitable, 150
writing personal essays, 94–97

About the Author

 **Lauren Porosoff** is the founder of EMPOWER Forwards, a collaborative consultancy practice that builds learning communities that truly belong to everyone and where everyone truly belongs. An educator since 2000, Lauren has taught at the Ethical Culture Fieldston School in the Bronx, New York; the Maret School in Washington, DC; and the Charles E. Smith Jewish Day School in Rockville, Maryland. She has taught 2nd, 5th, 6th, and 7th grade, mostly in English and history, and has also served as a DEI coordinator, grade dean, and leader of curricular initiatives.

Lauren's commitment to transforming the psychological experience of school has been a constant in her teaching practice, leading her to learn about values-guided behavior change in contextual psychology. Informed by research and practices from this field, and by her 18 years as a classroom teacher, Lauren develops tools and protocols that empower students and teachers to make school a source of meaning, vitality, and community. Her work includes the instructional design processes she describes in her book

Teach Meaningful: Tools to Design the Curriculum at Your Core (2020), the professional learning strategies in *The PD Curator: How to Design Peer-to-Peer Professional Learning That Elevates Teachers and Teaching* (2021), and the approaches to social-emotional learning in *EMPOWER Your Students: Tools to Inspire a Meaningful School Experience* (2018), *Two for-One Teaching: Connecting Instruction to Student Values* (2020), and *EMPOWER Moves for Social-Emotional Learning: Tools and Strategies to Evoke Student Values* (2022).

Lauren lives in New York with her co-everything Jonathan Weinstein, their two children, and a cat named Benedict. Learn more about Lauren's work at empowerforwards.com, or follow her on Twitter @LaurenPorosoff.

Related ASCD Resources: Student Engagement

At the time of publication, the following resources were available (ASCD stock numbers in parentheses).

Engaging Students in Every Classroom (QRG) by Susan Hentz and Michelle Vacchio (#QRG120056)

Fostering Resilient Learners: Strategies for Creating a Trauma-Sensitive Classroom by Kristin Van Marter Souers and Pete Hall (#116014)

Hanging In: Strategies for Teaching the Students Who Challenge Us Most by Jeffrey Benson (#114013)

How to Reach the Hard to Teach: Excellent Instruction for Those Who Need It Most by Jana Echevarría, Nancy Frey, and Douglas Fisher (#116010)

The PD Curator: How to Design Peer-to-Peer Professional Learning That Elevates Teachers and Teaching by Lauren Porosoff (#121029)

Questioning for Formative Feedback: Meaningful Dialogue to Improve Learning by Jackie Acree Walsh (#119006)

Relationship, Responsibility, and Regulation: Trauma-Invested Practices for Fostering Resilient Learners by Kristin Van Marter Souers and Pete Hall (#119027)

Teaching in the Fast Lane: How to Create Active Learning Experiences by Suzy Pepper Rollins (#117024)

Teaching to Strengths: Supporting Students Living with Trauma, Violence, and Chronic Stress by Debbie Zacarian, Lourdes Alvarez-Ortiz, and Judie Haynes (#117035)

Trauma-Invested Practices to Meet Students' Needs (QRG) by Kristin Van Marter Souers and Pete Hall (#QRG119077)

We Belong: 50 Strategies to Create Community and Revolutionize Classroom Management by Laurie Barron and Patti Kinney (#122002)

For up-to-date information about ASCD resources, go to www.ascd.org. You can search the complete archives of *Educational Leadership* at www.ascd.org/el.

ASCD myTeachSource®

Download resources from a professional learning platform with hundreds of research-based best practices and tools for your classroom at https://myteachsource.ascd.org.

For more information, send an email to member@ascd.org; call 1-800-933-2723 or 703-578-9600; send a fax to 703-575-5400; or write to Information Services, ASCD, 2800 Shirlington Rd., Suite 1001, Arlington, VA 22206 USA.